THE LITTLE BOOK OF

Wine

Daniel Le Conte des Floris
Éric Riewer
Tamara Thorgevsky
Pierre-Émile Durand

Flammarion

Inside front cover:

• Guide to French AOC Wines

Inside back cover:

• Wine-producing areas in France

and worldwide

Alphabetical Guide

Entries are arranged alphabetically into the following three sections.
(Each section is indicated by a color code.)

■ A Wine World Tour

Alsace	Domaine, Clos and Château	Loire Valley
Australia	Fraternities	Provence and Corsica
Beaujolais	Gaul	Rhône Valley
Bordeaux	Germany	South Africa
Burgundy	Highways and Byways	South America
Champagne	Italy	Southwest France
Classification	Jura and Savoy	Spain
Collecting	Languedoc-Roussillon	United States

■ The Rules of the Winegrower's Art

Aging	Oenology	Terroir
Aromatic and Flavored Wines	Organic Wine	Varieties
Blending	Origins	Vine Life Cycle
Bottles	Production	Vinegar
Climate	Pruning	Vinification
Disease	Red Wine	Vins Doux Naturels
Fermentation	Reference Books	Vintage Years
Fortified Wines	Rosé Wine	White Wine
Harvest	Soil	Wine-making
Liqueur Wines	Sommelier	and Maturation
Oak	Sparkling Wines	

■ The Wine Lover's Guide

Ancient World	French Revolution	Prices
Aphrodisiac	Glasses	Purchase
Cellar	Health	Renaissance
Consumption	Labels	Vocabulary
Cuisine	Literature	Wine Bars
Decanters	Middle Ages	Wine Fairs
Dionysus	Mythology	Wine Shops, Taverns,
Drinking Songs	Nineteenth Century	and Guinguettes
Drunkenness	Opening Wine, and Serving	Wine Tours
Eighteenth Century	Temperature	
Eucharist	Paintings	

Cross references to other entries are marked with an asterisk.

THE STORY OF WINE

As the new millennium opens, the odyssey of wine continues. Our story begins before written history itself, though never before has the humble grape been tasted, discussed and analyzed to the extent it is today. And so, before we gaze into our crystal ball at the future of wine, it would be well worthwhile to take a quick glimpse into its past.

The Odyssey of Wine

The best-known wine-producing region in the world, the cradle of the wine business itself, Bordeaux*, has been sending ships laden with wine to all points of the compass from time immemorial. Throughout history, Bordeaux has been considered without equal in terms of the quality and the quantity of its produce. Today, however, it is beginning to look rather nervously over its shoulder at some newly emerging wine-producing nations and up-and-coming French regions. The final VINEXPO of the twentieth century— wine's world trade fair which takes place in Bordeaux every two years—brought the dynamism of the whole industry into vivid focus and showed just how strongly some sectors have been pushing for a "new deal" in the wine market.

Au Bon Climat, a Californian wine.

Some wine lovers have even dared to say that it is possible to unearth varietals* offering better value for money than minor Bordeaux wines. Even a monument such as the 1855 *classement* (classification)* of Bordeaux growths has been shaken to its foundations by the latest developments: the price* of Médoc *premiers crus* (first growths) is now exceeded on a regular basis by a number of "opportunists" from districts that have not received the famous classification, such as Château de Valandraud (Saint-Émilion), Château Le Pin (Pomerol), and even by bottles* from the New World, such as Colgin, Screaming Eagle, or Marcassin, which have been known to steal the limelight at wine auctions.

Preceding double page: Pierre Victor Olagnon, *Vineyard Owner Visiting his Winery*, (detail), 1829, Oil on canvas. Musée du Vin de Bourgogne, Beaune, France.

Moreover, the soaring prices of the major growths over the last few years (even in the case of vintages* of questionable quality) seem to have put an end to the special place the Bordeaux area has in the wine-lover's heart. The public is more inclined than ever to explore off the beaten track of Bordeaux and Burgundy*, and to seek out less well-trodden paths such as Languedoc-Roussillon* in France, as well as Spain*, the United States*, and South America*.

carafe wine

Over the last few years, a number of regions with age-old winery traditions have gained favor with even the French wine lover, who until recently was held back by a number of dubious prejudices (the Languedoc region's history of producing red "carafe wine"*, or Spain's oxidized and high-alcohol produce, for example), as have more recent wine-making history in areas such as Chile or California, which are often suspected of offering nothing but a pale reflection of French wine know-how.

The cellar-master testing wine at Château Lagrezette, in Cahors, south-western France.

In fact, the change in attitude is an indirect consequence of a dual evolution in the technical and economic spheres, linked in part to the development of modern oenology* and in part to an upsurge in demand for quality wine, though in fact neither of these factors wholly accounts for the complexities of what has really been a sea-change in wine consumption*.

New Techniques in Old Terroirs

The significance of the technological advances of the last two decades can hardly be overstated. Progress now presents growers with a wide range of options for honing their skills, both in the vineyard and in the cellar. First of all, they have greater control over wine-growing and a better understanding of what makes for a good harvest* (both in terms of ripeness and plant health), making it feasible to optimize the quality of the raw material—the grape. The techniques used by the winemakers themselves in the context of

Pruned vine branches being burnt in the vineyard at Savigny-lès-Beaune, Côte de Beaune, eastern France

9

Racking off the lees from a vat, in the Bordeaux region.

an ever wider global wine market have led to valuable lessons in vinification*. The best winegrowers have benefited greatly from these advances, improving the quality of their wine considerably.

Today, mistakes in vinification have become much rarer, and poor vintages are few and far between. The vast range of techniques for "correcting" or "improving" a wine can now make good a mistake or save an entire harvest during particularly mediocre years.

It should be borne in mind, however, that these advances are not without their downside. It has become relatively easy to produce what some have justifiably dubbed "high-tech" wines. These are acceptable in terms of industrial production but do not give the essence of particular *terroirs**, and fail to bring out the typical flavor of the soil on which the vine grows.

Tradition and Innovation

The demand for quality has never been so strong. A new generation of winegrowers, passionate about their craft and open to ideas, now rely as much on tradition as on scientific progress. Yet this long overdue renaissance in traditional methods and the adoption of effective new techniques has its dangers too. The quest for technically perfect wines may lead to nondescript results: the future would be bleak indeed for wine lovers if all wines were "good," but tasted alike. France's long tradition of winemaking and its dominant market position offer an interesting case. On one side is the sometimes inflexible authority of the INAO (*Institut National des Appellations d'Origine*) which selects growths for the honor of appellation using a list of specifications that applies as much to the geographical limits of the *terroir* or field concerned, as to the way the vines are looked after, the selection of variety*, and *élevage* (wine-making*), etc. On the other side, there are the winegrowers themselves. The most demanding strive to bring out the finest qualities of their *terroir* in the most effective and original manner, above and beyond its time-honored characteristics. The boldest of all seek to produce wine that is better adapted to public taste and thus counter competition from countries without such strict rules. For it should not be forgotten that the INAO was set up in the 1930s to save French wine-growing from anarchic production methods and wholesale trafficking, and that it still carries the flag for *terroir* wines at a time when varietals (the French *vins de cépage*) are severing all links with their place of origin.

Australian wine. Henschke, Julius 1997, Eden Valley Riesling.

It should thus be possible to reach beyond the demands of the rule-book—which gives structure to wine production and thus reduces the likelihood of producing mediocre or even bad wines—to the energy of the visionaries who have opened new frontiers in winemaking, such as Éloi Dürrbach at the Domaine de Trévallon in Les Baux-de-Provence, Jean Thevenet at the Domaine de La Bongran in the Mâcon region, or Jean-Michel Deiss in Alsace*, to name some of the most notable figures.

The Global Market

Although global production* is on an upward trend, the vogue for wine among the public at large has gone hand in hand with a decrease in overall consumption*. The preference is now to drink less, but of higher quality. The abiding fear of the wine lover is of being submerged beneath a tidal wave of mediocrity due to overproduction. No-one has yet devised a "formula" attractive to every consumer worldwide, even though some household names have set great store by alliances designed to guarantee them a fair slice of any future market. Mondavi from California has joined forces with three well-known names: Château Mouton-Rothschild, to create a wine christened "Opus One," with Frescobaldi in Italy* for "Luce," and with Errazuriz in Chile for "Sena." The same

Mouton-Rothschild has formed a joint-venture with Concha y Toro, also in Chile, and produced "Almaviva." The Italian Antinori has forged links with an estate in Washington State.

Modern oenology (wine science) has of course been a crucial factor in the quality revolution, but the role of marketing should not be understated either, especially when it entails the realization on the part of producers that "quality pays,"… and indeed it pays handsomely on occasion, as one can see from the sky-high prices attained by top wines from every producing country. This phenomenon has affected not only Bordeaux but also *premier cru* Burgundy, and the *grands crus* Hermitage and Côte-Rôtie from the Rhône valley*, Rieslings from Germany's Mosel valley* (Egon Müller's sublime Trockenbeernauslese), exceptional Tuscan wines such as Sassicaia or the great Barolo from Piedmont in Italy, the Vega Sicilia from Spain and finally, New World wines such as Diamond Creek from California's Napa Valley, or Henschke's Hill of Grace from Australia*.

Hardly a year passes without some new "great wine" hitting the market. The increasingly demanding and ever-inquisitive consumer also plays a key role in the spiraling quality of wine. A plethora of wine bars*, wine-tasting courses and wine clubs, specialized journals and TV shows slake the public thirst and, each in their own way, contribute to its continued progress. As the wine historian Marcel Lachiver put it: "It is obvious there can be no great wines without enlightened consumers."

What is a Great Wine?

The Australian writer and winegrower James Halliday has often said that wine is there to give pleasure and not to be worshipped. It is difficult, however, not to succumb to the veneration inspired by such mythical names as Romanée-Conti, Pétrus, or Yquem. Without wishing to destroy the myth, is there any straightforward way of understanding just what makes a *grand vin* great?

Growers gladly concede that a great wine is born from a combination of *cépage* (variety), soil*, climate*, and the care lavished on the grapes on the vine and in the cellar. They remind us, too, of the importance of human intervention in the equation, in order to bring out the best from the *terroir*. Many have been disappointed in the past by wines from celebrated appellations, such as Vosne-Romanée and Margaux, which were not nurtured with sufficient care.

The toughest thing is to find the right *terroir*. If it is true that Europe has indeed stolen a march on its New World rivals, it is

Vineyard in Australia.

mainly thanks to its centuries-long search for adequate *terroirs* based on trial-and-error combinations of grape varieties that bring out the best in the character of the chosen soil and location. This quest for the balance between "varietal" and "soil" is now becoming most apparent in those countries which at the outset doubted the usefulness of the whole notion of *terroir*. The Napa Valley in California has pushed the individual characteristics of sub-appellations such as Oakville and Rutherford, whereas in Australia the Coonawarra region is much feted for its red soil, a good vehicle for Cabernet sauvignon.

In this age of marketing that tends to put its money on varietals in an effort to attract consumers, it is important to stress that it is impossible to produce a great wine from just any old grape variety. The list is today limited to those which offer potential complexity and are capable of aging* well: Cabernet sauvignon, Chardonnay, Merlot, Nebbiolo, Pinot noir, Riesling, and Syrah feature on the hallowed list, though this does not necessarily exclude the possibility that at some future date some other name might not join them. Another basic tenet is that there is scarcely a single great wine that is not matured in oak casks*.

Unfortunately, the oak cask is no longer exclusively used for wines of sufficient body to absorb the aroma of the wood without being overwhelmed. The woody flavors that some consumers hold so dear in fact obscures the cask's true role.

The potential for aging—by which we mean the capacity to increase in complexity over time, not just to survive—is enhanced by carefully controlled oxidation when the wine is maturing in cask (see Wine-making and Maturing). It contributes to the complex alchemical process between certain components of the wood and of the grapes, such as tannins, anthocyans (the compounds that impart the color), and alcohol. It is only after their gradual transformation in the bottle that a wine can do itself justice and release the inimitable bouquet that comes from successful aging.

Alongside the rare *crus* that have this capacity, countless failures—wines that are oxidized, ruined, or rotten—lie in cellars, kept too long by people who persist in believing that all wines improve with age, whereas in fact this is the case only with a chosen few.

And Bordeaux?

Our whirlwind tour through the world of wine ends back where it started, in Bordeaux. It may be given to this generation to see the end of this famed region's golden age, and even perhaps to witness the gradual overthrow of the now only relative supremacy of French wine (the case of Bordeaux being symptomatic of a more general situation). What is sure (and the recent history of wine bears this out) is that no single region has a monopoly of the best wine-growing areas, and still less of winemaking know-how. On the last point, it should be noted, however, that it is still in French universities that the top oenologists for the new wine-producing nations study, and in the best French vineyards that growers learn their trade.

Nonetheless, Bordeaux has overcome many an obstacle in the course of its long history. It will no doubt keep its supremacy for a good few years yet, for at least two reasons which can, in theory, be transplanted to any other region intent on producing wine of quality and character. The first is that, in spite of an enduring reputation for conservatism, the people of Bordeaux have, over time, learnt how to renew and adapt their wine-growing and winemaking methods and thus to optimize the quality of their product. Improvements include the introduction of drainage, of pruning according to the "Guyot" method that results in superior vine development, the use of *bouillie bordelaise* or "Bordeaux mixture" containing lime, copper sulfate and water to combat the disease* of mildew, or, more recently still, techniques of reverse osmosis so as to increase the concentration of must (grape juice before fermentation is complete) after a wet harvest. Even if a winemaker like Robert Mondavi from California could say that, during the 1960s, a number of great Bordeaux estates were resting on their laurels, oenologists such as Émile Peynaud have managed to put an end to this gradual decline by devising a list of procedures that respect the specific qualities of each château while encouraging the healthy practice of pooling ideas.

The second reason for the continuing supremacy of Bordeaux wines is the extraordinary diversity of *terroirs* and the no less great variety of styles encountered among the 57 appellations and upwards of 114,000 hectares of grape vines cultivated in the Bordeaux region. Even if, for commercial reasons, a large proportion of world wine production is lean-

Traditional bottle-turning racks (*pupitres*) at the Roederer champagne cellars, Rheims (Champagne region).

ing towards varietals (made of one variety of grape), Bordeaux, under the stern eye of the INAO, knows how to bring out all the flavor of its blended wines*. Moreover, as globalization gathers pace, smoothing out local particularities, Bordeaux (with other regions such as Burgundy, the Rhône Valley, and Languedoc-Roussillon) is set upon reminding consumers that the same varieties planted in different conditions give very different wines.

In the twenty-first century, it will be the consumer with the intelligence and initiative to vary his drinking pleasure by exploring the world of wine in all its diversity who, like the wise and fortunate Ulysses, will journey the farthest and the best.

Éric RIEWER and Daniel LE CONTE DES FLORIS

■ Aging

In truth, wines that are good for "laying down" —that is to say which improve with age in the bottle—are few and far between. Depending on the quality of the vintage* concerned, some fine wines require five or six years to settle down, while others need ten or even fifteen years to express their character to the full. Not everyone is lucky enough to have a good cellar*, however, and if wines are badly stored they age prematurely. The phenomenon of aging is not well understood. It probably results from a whole series of combinations between the alcohols, acids, and polyphenols (tannins and pigments) that take place in the reduced (i.e. non-oxygenated) atmosphere of a firmly corked bottle. Among the factors that promote a wine's longevity, the crucial ones seem to be acidity, above all for wines from northern climes, and the degree of alcohol for those from the south. During aging, the "robe" (color) of red wines* becomes less intense and evolves from a violet overtone to a more orangey hue. The "nose" of the wine gradually loses its primary (connected to the grape) and secondary aromas (derived from fermentation*), and is changed into tertiary aromas (linked to the changes that take place in an enclosed space) that are known as the "bouquet" (undergrowth, game, fruit eau-de-vie, etc.). In the mouth the taste of the wine increases in suppleness, the tannins dissolve, and the astringency decreases. When too old, however, the nose becomes "fizzy"—although sometimes with a certain finesse—a red wine turns brownish, and tastes tired and acidic. Some great white wines* from Burgundy* or the Rhône* also deserve to be laid down for ten or so years. As for *vin jaune* from the Jura, it seems to last forever. DLCDF

Augé wine merchant's, Paris.

A bottle of Rioja Marquès de Riscal dating from 1875.

■ ALSACE : *white wine growing areas*

Alsace is the great French white wine-growing area. Running down a thin strip over some 13,000 hectares that stretches from Strasbourg in the north to Mulhouse in the south, its unique features derive from its northern situation (with Champagne, it is the most northerly French wine-producing region).

The climate* is extremely hot in the summer and extremely cold in the winter and there is relatively modest rainfall since the clouds tend to strike the mountains of the Vosges, which border the entire area. Some *terroirs** have acquired an enviable reputation—

Andlau, Baar, Kaysersberg, Bergheim, etc.—and produce wines of rare quality. Fifty localities were classified in the mid-1970s and have the right to label themselves *"Alsace Grand Cru,"* if the variety chosen is Riesling, Gewürztraminer, Pinot Gris, or Muscat. As against other French wine-growing areas, that lay great importance on their *terroir*, Alsace's production is generally organized by grape varieties. Other indications regarding liqueur wines* include *vendanges tardives*, ("late vintage") if the grapes are left for optimum ripening, and *sélection de grains nobles*, ("selection of noble grapes")

Village and vineyard in Hunawihr, Alsace.

[handwritten annotations: Muscat: asparagus / gewürztraminer: exotic dishes]

if they are also enriched by noble rot. Alsace wines are varied enough to be an accompaniment to the whole meal. The lightness of Sylvaner is increasingly being ousted by a Pinot blanc of more regular quality that can be served as an aperitif or with simpler dishes. Fruity Muscat goes well with asparagus, while the Gewürztraminer is really spicy and can hold its own against even the most pungent cheeses as well as exotic dishes. Pinot gris, occasionally still known as Tokay, can also give some fabulous liqueur wines* when fine weather allows a late harvest. And last but not least, there is Riesling, a magnificent accompaniment to any classic recipe based on fish, and the only wine (apart from those made from "late vintaged" grapes or from *sélection de grains nobles*) to benefit from a relatively lengthy aging* process. The two major drawbacks with Alsace wines are dilution, due to its massive yields, and the residual sugars that can make the wine cloying when fermentation* has been halted prematurely. Vigilance is the watchword here, and one should steer clear of wines that are both light and sugary, as it is difficult to find dishes that go with them. DLCDF and PÉD

Banquet scene (detail) from the tomb fresco known as *The Diver*, found at Paestum, 480 B.C. Museo Archeologico Nazionale, Paestum.

■ Ancient World

Without the fearless seafarers of antiquity, wine would never have arrived from Egypt or Phoenicia in Crete, and thence to Greece around 1500 B.C., and then on to Sicily and southern Italy, an area where the vine flourished so profitably that it was later dubbed Oenotria, the "land of wine." The main exporters were the islands of the Aegean Sea, the wines of Khios and Lesbos being among the most highly prized. Full-bodied, and renowned for sweetness—the scene of ripe grapes drying in the sun is described by Homer—stored in jars or transported in amphorae, these wines were never taken straight. Mixed with lashings of seawater in a metal *krater*, sometimes with herbs and spices added, they were served in wine-cups at the *symposion*, the post-prandial debate with which Greek banquets drew to a close. The Romans took up the mantle in the first century B.C.,

and made further developments in wine-growing. Preferring white wine*, they even blanched other types with sulfur vapor. Filtered through straw baskets, the must was left to ferment in earthenware vessels before being "fined" (clarified) with plaster, ash, or potter's clay, but also, as is done today, with fish-glue or gelatin. The prevailing fashion was for mulled wine (*defrutum*) with added honey (*mulsum*), or peppered, perfumed with herbs or resin, and served cut with seawater. The common people and the army drank coarse draft wine, or *posca*, with a vinegar* base.

Initially, women were forbidden from drinking, on pain of death. Wine did indeed lead to a degree of looseness (see Aphrodisiac), though by no means all banquets ended in an orgy. Roman taste underwent a decisive change on the arrival of lighter wines from Gaul* and northern Italy. TT

■ Aphrodisiac

The fruit of a mysterious process called fermentation*, associated with drunkenness, blood and Dionysiac* excesses, wine was long considered a menace to female virtue. In Roman legend, Orpheus was torn apart by a horde of women crazed by wine and desire. In ancient Greece, women, with the exception of dancing-girls and musicians, were banned from banquets. The Romans would even kiss their wives on the mouth to smell their breath. "If you catch your wife drinking wine," Cato the Censor urged, "kill her!" Under the Empire, however, Roman women were eventually allowed to drink wine. Throughout history, periods of pagan and humanist celebration of wine have been succeeded by more moralistic times (see Middle Ages), while the Church and philosophers from Plato to Montaigne praised moderation in all things. Only in the seventeenth century did the idea that love and wine were mutually exclusive recede, while the eighteenth century* disposed of the age-old belief that once wine was drunk it immediately changed into blood. Venus and Bacchus were henceforth inseparable, and love-making among the aristocracy and common people alike provided opportunities to down champagne* or claret. Wine has always provoked a certain distrust, however, as the Porter in Macbeth (II, 2, 26-28) put it, in his ambivalent paean to wine: "Lechery, sir, it provokes and unprovokes; it provokes the desire but takes away the performance." TT

Titian,
Bacchanal of the Andrians,
1523–24.
Oil on canvas.
Museo del
Prado, Madrid.

Retsina : Greece

Aromatic and Flavored Wines

Flavored and aromatic wines were already much prized in the ancient world*. They are made from fortified wine*, that is to say, unfermented or partially fermented grape juice to which alcohol has been added prior to or during fermentation*. They are then steeped in various aromatic flavorings (plants, spices, fruit, and so forth) so as to obtain wines of a particular flavor, some of which were highly regarded historically for their medicinal qualities. The most famous of all, vermouth, has been known since at least the sixteenth century. It contains wormwood (*Wermut* in German, hence the name), and other bitter-tasting herbs, and in today's mass-produced form it is marketed under a host of brand names: Martini, Noilly Prat, Cinzano, Dubonnet, Chambéry, etc.

Absinthe, a similar drink, has been banned in Europe for many years after it was found to cause insanity if drunk in large quantities. Absinthe is said to be the cause of van Gogh's madness, driving him to cut off his ear.

Retsina, the Greek wine flavored with pine resin, is another example of a popular aromatized wine. The present debate over the use of wood-shavings as a flavoring additive in wines that have not been matured in cask has itself almost given rise to a new type of aromatic wine. ER

Two examples of Élixir de Carthagène, wines flavored with spices, by Chantal Comte.

■ Australia

Australia is what is known as a "New World" producer, as compared to the old European countries. The first vines appeared at the time of British colonization, at the end of the eighteenth century*. The first vineyard worthy of the name was planted near Sydney in the middle of the nineteenth century*. In the absence of any wine-growing tradition, the Australians resorted to a pragmatic approach, scouring the land for cooler and wetter zones (along rivers), and experimenting with varieties* of every origin: Riesling, Sémillon, Chardonnay, and Sauvignon, for whites*; Syrah and Cabernet varieties for reds*.

Having installed irrigation systems (a practice prohibited in France) and with mechanized production compensating for a lack of manpower, Australia is now undergoing the process of identifying different *terroirs** along French lines. The finest wine-growing regions are Coonawarra (the "Australian Médoc"), Barossa Valley (with superb Syrahs), Margaret River (where the climate* resembles that of the Bordeaux region), and the Hunter Valley (the earliest historic vineyards). Their varietals* are straightforward and fruity and have won a devoted following among consumers. DLCDF

Vineyard at Coldstream Hills, Yarra Valley, Australia.

■ BEAUJOLAIS

The yearly launch of "Beaujolais Nouveau" on the third Thursday in November accompanied by media coverage from all over the world has earned this region a certain reputation. The success of this ingenious commercial and technical tour de force—producing, bottling, and distributing a fruity, fresh, and quaffable wine all over the world—is impressive: more than half the entire harvest is sold before the year is out! These wines are supple with not much tannin and a fruity aroma with a touch of "pear drops" (acetone aroma), and can sometimes be heady due to the short time that the whole grapes are in contact with the crusher in the closed vats.

The wine-growing countryside is hilly and stretches from Mâcon—the south of the Burgundy area to which it was at one time attached—to Lyon, which marks the northernmost tip of the Rhône area. The continental climate* has a Mediterranean influence (hard winters, devastating frosts, early springs occasionally followed by nippy frosts, and torrid, if often stormy summers). The only grape used is the Gamay noir à jus blanc variety that gives white juice, a fairly vigorous plant that has to be pruned back hard to prevent the rootstocks being exhausted and the wine ending up watery. The very few white wines* come from Chardonnay and Aligoté.

The vineyards cover around 22,000 hectares and are divided into three areas. The chalky limestone and sedimentary soil* to the west and south correspond to the regional "Beaujolais" appellation. The metamorphic granite rocks comprise the "Beaujolais-Villages," and ten growths: Brouilly, Côte-de-Brouilly, Chenas, Chiroubles, Fleurie, Juliénas, Morgon (which acquires a woody, raspberry flavor thanks probably to the presence of manganese on its *terroir**), Moulin-à-Vent (the king of Beaujolais, a wine to

Beaujolais *crus*.

lay down), Régnié (the last to have acquired the appellation), and Saint-Amour. Most often, Beaujolais is an easy-drinking wine that goes well with cold meats and cheese, but the best *crus* can accompany grander fare just as well as Burgundy*, which they sometimes come to resemble as they age. A regrettable if time-honored custom allows for the declassification of certain growths of Beaujolais and their labeling with the Burgundy appellation, whereas the latter are made from Pinot noir. DLCDF and PÉD

27

"Cain Five,"
wine blended from
five varieties. Santa
Helena estate,
Napa Valley,
California.

■ BLENDING
One or more varieties

Whereas varietal wines are vinified* from a single (or dominant) grape variety, blended wines are made from a number of grape types. In France, little was made of this distinction until about twenty years ago, but it has developed there in the wake of commercial success elsewhere. In the United States and other parts of the world, the label carries the name of the grape variety. In France, the INAO has always been against the naming of the varieties on *appellation d'Origine* wine bottles (except those from Alsace*) so as to place the emphasis on the growing area or *terroir*.

Blending from various vats in the winery allows the production of wine of a uniform quality and style in worthwhile quantities. In fact, the same estate or domaine* can contain plots belonging to different *terroirs*, or that are planted with vines of various ages, that produce vats with distinctive characters.

Although today's trend is to emphasize this character in small-scale vats, blending is particularly crucial for the great Bordeaux châteaux, that use the contents of their best vats for their headline wines and keep back the others for a second or even third label. Champagne* is the blended wine par excellence. It is often produced from three varieties, and even blended from different years, in the case of non-vintage dry wines. ER

Bunches of Syrah
grapes, in the
Côte-Rôtie region
of France.

■ BORDEAUX

This most famous of all the world's vineyards grew up around the estuary formed by the rivers Gironde, Garonne, and Dordogne. In a way, the Bordeaux region owes its wine to its waters. Grown on predominantly gravelly soil soothed by the rivers and the sea, and sheltered by a coastal screen of pine-trees, Bordeaux wine was first shipped to England as early as the twelfth century, and it is to the British that it owes a significant proportion of its fame. It was only in the seventeenth century, however, that its great estates came into their own. Thanks to a careful choice of vineyards,

to the control exerted over the yield, and to the maturing of the wine in casks, durable links have been forged between *terroirs*, châteaux,—and renown.

The resulting hierarchy gave rise to the classification* of the reds* of Médoc and the liqueur* or dessert wines of Sauternes enshrined in the authoritative 1855 *classement*, still applied today. It recognized four red first growths (*premiers crus*), Margaux, Latour, Lafite-Rothschild, and Haut-Brion (this last in fact belongs to the Graves zone) and a single white exceptional first growth*, Yquem. Only much later, in 1973, were

Château Pichon-Baron and its vineyard at Pauillac in the Médoc.

these joined by Mouton Rothschild, at which time Saint-Émilion too obtained the right to its own classification.

Yet Bordeaux is not necessarily synonymous with grands crus and expensive wines (see Prices). Sheltering behind the elite lurk millions of bottles that take advantage of the Bordeaux name and find their way onto dining-tables all over the world. Fifty-seven different appellations share the approximately 500 million liters a year that are produced from over 110,000 hectares. Over such a vast area, soil* conditions are obviously very diverse, but it is, above all, in well-drained vineyards that the best *crus* are to be found, alluvial soil being the reserve of wines labeled simply appellation "Bordeaux."

The common factor among all Bordeaux wines is the careful way in which they are blended from a number of varieties (see Blending). The tannic varieties Cabernet sauvignon and Cabernet franc make the reds suitable for laying down, while the more supple Merlot contributes a velvety touch. As to the whites, the lively Sauvignon grape complements the more delicate Sémillon and Muscadelle, which are prone to the noble rot that produces the liqueur wines. DLCDF and PÉD

31

Bottles

Wood, earthenware, glass—there are in fact only a few materials appropriate for the storage of wine. A Canaanite invention introduced into Egypt around 1500 B.C., the earthenware amphora is proofed with a layer of pitch or wax and stopped with plaster or cork before being sealed with pitch. The Greek amphora (see Ancient World) contained approximately 40 liters and the Roman 26—around 35 present-day bottles. Well sealed, an amphora was as airtight as a bottle and the wine inside could survive for a long time with no ill effect.

Light yet durable, the chestnut or oak* barrel used by the Celts first appeared for transporting beer. Around the third century, however, it progressively began to replace the amphora. Unfortunately it is not airtight, and so the pleasures of aged vintages* vanished with it (see Middle Ages). The original Syrian technique of glass-blowing had been widespread since the first century B.C., but the material was mainly used for making decanters* and goblets. Only in the seventeenth century, with the English invention of coal-fired furnaces

Relief showing amphorae being stored in a cellar. Second or third century A.D. Museo della Civiltà Romana, Rome.

to fire glass, did the heyday of fragile white glass made with wood-fired furnaces come to an end (see Eighteenth Century). The new, strong and stable English bottles were to revolutionize the way wine was stored and drunk. Their necks were also reinforced with a ring, which allowed a return to cork stoppers. Today's bottle contains an international standard of 0.75 liters, but the main French shapes still survive (such as Champagne, Alsace, Burgundy, etc.), while the elegant Bordeaux bottle has been copied the world over.

It should be noted that the shape of the bottle has some influence over the development of the wine within: the larger the container, the longer it takes to mature. The ideal volume seems to be the magnum of 1.5 liters. Beyond that size lies the realm of generously proportioned vessels with Biblical names: Jeroboam, Mathusalem, Salmanzar, Nebuchadnezzar. Their volume varies according to region, however: the Champagne Jeroboam (3 liters) is not the same size as the Bordeaux variety (4.5 liters). TT

■ BURGUNDY

The amazing vineyards of Burgundy are extraordinarily varied. Homogenous thanks to the single varieties of grape planted (Pinot noir in the case of the reds*, and Chardonnay for the white*), yet distinctive thanks to the diversity in the soil* and subsoil of the region, and to the appellations they produce: almost a hundred over 28,000 hectares (comprising 3 percent of all French arable land under vine). More than anywhere else, the notion of *terroir** here acquires its full meaning, as the slightest difference in exposure, altitude, or in soil type can result in a potentially very different wine. The hallowed ridge running from Dijon to Chagny produces great wines whose names alone set one dreaming. Over forty kilometers, the slender strip of the Côte de Nuits, already noted in the Middle Ages*, comprises a complex patchwork of tiny plots (here often known as *climats*) that give rise to excellent reds. One can go from the vineyards of Clos de Bèze to Cambertin, from Musigny to Clos de Vougeot, or from Romanée-Saint-Vivant to Romanée-Conti, without noticing. Further south lies Côte de Beaune, the *domaine* of great white wines* such as Corton-Charlemagne, Meursault, Montrachet, etc.

The prices such wines reach being in keeping with their fame, it is no surprise that many New World countries have tried to acclimatize the two Burgundy varieties to their own conditions, with, it should be said, a measure of success as regards Chardonnay.

Luckily, there are still a few Burgundy wines to be found at reasonable prices. To the northwest of Dijon, the Chablis area (more than 5,000 hectares) provides lively dry wines whose grands crus and even some *premiers crus* are often drunk too young, the optimum wait being at least five years. The reputation of Chablis abroad has been rock solid for decades. To the south of Chagny lies the Côte Châlonnaise, mainly devoted to reds (Rully, Mercurey, Givry, etc.) followed by the Mâconnais, noted for its everyday drinking (Mâcon-Village) or the grand (Pouilly-Fuissé) whites.

Like all wines, most Burgundies are drinkable after a couple of years, whereas the first growths call for from three to five years of bottle-aging, and the great growths anything from six to eight. Connoisseurs of special vintages* who have a large cellar can afford the risk of keeping them back for a bit longer and thus savor, if they are lucky, the finesse and incredible complexity of a twenty-year-old *grand cru*. DLCDF and PÉD

"Sorrow can be alleviated by good sleep, a bath and a glass of good wine."

Saint Thomas Aquinas

Vintage at Grands-Échézeaux,
Domaine de la Romanée-Conti,
Côte de Nuits.

■ Cellar

Your wine collection* is starting to grow, and exceeds the space available. You need to find a suitable place to lay down your bottles*. Unfortunately, this can be a real headache, since the ideal conditions for storage are difficult to achieve in a modern apartment. A cellar should remain cool, of course, but a temperature between 42–62°F (8–17°C) is acceptable if there are no abrupt changes, which tire the wine and reduce its potential "bouquet." Nonetheless, the wine will age more rapidly and less smoothly in temperatures nearing 62°F (17°C). The ideal is a stable temperature of 51–53°F (11–12°C) and high humidity (between 70 and 80 percent) to prevent the cork drying out. Finally, the place chosen should be sheltered from the light (crucial for champagne*), from vibration (a problem with cellars near subway transportation systems), and above all from materials with a penetrating odor (household products, paint, shoe-polish, vegetables, and so on).

A prefabricated wine-cellar designed to be buried in the ground can be installed in houses that have no adequate space of their own. If there is no cellar at all, wine cupboards present a solution for smaller collections of up to 260 bottles (though versions with space for 1,000 do exist). Finally, if one is not averse to "boarding out" one's bottles, one can always hire a space in a communal cellar which, in theory, should possess ideal storage conditions. ER

Three prestigious French wines: Saint-Julien Château Beychevelle, Chambolle-Musigny from Domaine de Grivalet, and Barsac Château-Coutet.

Drouin cellars, Beaune, Burgundy.

■ CHAMPAGNE

The quality of the wines from the Champagne region was acknowledged as early as the ninth century, and no French king was ever crowned without champagne being drunk. Until the sixteenth century it was only the red* vin d'Aÿ that was valued. In 1688, a certain Dom Pérignon (1638–1715) became cellar master at the Abbey at Hautvilliers. He did not in fact invent champagne bubbles, but the stricter methods he introduced to the wine-making process brought considerable progress. In the nineteenth century*, technical improvements and the demands of the English market for a drier wine resulted in today's champagne: the famous bubbles result from a second fermentation* in the bottle after sugar and yeast are added (see Sparkling Wines).

One of the strange things about champagne is that it is made by blending different varieties*, terroirs*, and even years. Of the three permitted cépages (the varieties of Pinot noir, Pinot meunier, and Chardonnay), two are red. Carefully controlled pressing produces a white must that is separated from the grape-skins. The expression blanc de blancs designates a champagne made exclusively from Chardonnay grapes. The vineyards number 320 crus, classed from 80 to 100 percent (the seventeen most renowned are known as "100 percent") depending on where the grapes come from. With few exceptions, a champagne owes its character to a whole mosaic of terroirs.

The brut sans année ("dry non-vintage") accounts for 70 percent of yield and is made up of the year's wine with the addition of a variable amount of earlier vintages* which help to keep the style of the bottled wine in spite of the vagaries of the weather. The champagne range also includes rosés* (pink champagne is the only wine allowed to be made by adding red wine to white), vintage wines (good years), prestigious cuvées spéciales, and sweeter demi-secs, etc.

Vintage or no, once sold, champagne should be drunk within a year—unless one is partial to the singular taste of old champagne. Being fragile and light-sensitive, champagne does not appreciate rough treatment and should therefore not be bought in supermarkets or stored for too long in the refrigerator. It is best drunk cold, but not ice-cold, from 46°F (8°C) for an ordinary wine up to 54°F (12°C) for a truly exceptional one. For dessert, demi-sec can be recommended. ππ

"I only drink champagne when I am happy, and when I'm sad. Sometimes I drink it when I'm alone. When I have company, I consider it obligatory. I trifle with it if I am not hungry and drink it when I am. Otherwise I never touch it—unless I'm thirsty."

Lily Bollinger, champagne heiress

Racks of white Charbant champagne.

■ CLASSIFICATION:
Crus and terroirs, domaines and estates

In an attempt to introduce a semblance of order to the huge abundance of wines dating back centuries, enlightened drinkers of every period have attempted to rank them in terms of quality. In Burgundy, the notion of the *cru* ("growth") has its origins in the mosaic of "*climats*" (areas) drawn up by Cistercian monks in the medieval period— and probably by the Romans and Celts before them. By the fourteenth century, the vineyards with the best location had been identified in the Jurançon region.

Vieux Château Certan
Grand Cru
POMEROL
1974
Appellation Pomerol contrôlée
SOCIÉTÉ CIVILE DU VIEUX CHATEAU CERTAN
Héritière de Mr et Mme Georges THIENPONT
PROPRIÉTAIRE A POMEROL · FRANCE   148 cl
MIS EN BOUTEILLE AU CHÂTEAU

The best known of all *classements* (classifications) is that governing Bordeaux, which was laid down in 1855 on the occasion of the Paris World Fair. The system of five classes of growths is limited to sixty châteaux in the Médoc region, to which has been added Haut-Brion, a Graves wine. The classification was drawn up by wine-merchants and brokers, not according to the quality of the wines concerned, but to their price*. Although its rigidity has been the butt of much criticism, the classification survives intact. Other Bordeaux appellations have devised similar, if more flexible, schemes. In 1955, Saint-Émilion set up its own classification which undergoes revision around every ten years (the most recent was in 1996). A neighboring appellation area, Pomerol, has never sought to receive a classification. Indeed, for many wine-merchants and consumers, the ratings allotted by certain wine critics have taken on more significance than *classement* proper.

In parallel, the INAO (*Institut National des Appellations d'Origine*, founded in 1935) has set up the AOC (*Appellation d'Origine Contrôlée*) and AOVDQS (*Appellation d'Origine de Vins Délimités de Qualité Supérieure*) categories to guarantee the authenticity of wines from different vineyards. So as to stress the notion of *terroir** and its typical character, this same organization has decreed regulations concerning geographical limits, permitted varieties, methods of wine-making*, etc.

Other countries have since adopted similar regimes: DOC— *Denominazione di Origine Controllata*—in Italy*, DO— *Denominación de Origen*—in Spain*. Today, the European Union has done the same with VQPRD, in English QWPSR (Quality Wine Produced in a Specific Region). ER

▨ CLIMATE: Water and Sun

Every vine-plant, and *Vitis vinifera* above all, hates frost. In spring, a temperature of 26°F (-3°C) is enough to nip the buds and to jeopardize the whole harvest. Combined with wind-chill and humidity, winter temperatures between 5 and -4°F (-15 and -20°C) can destroy the vines, and they have to be dug up. For these reasons, in Europe, the cultivated area under vines does not stretch to northern climes (above the fiftieth parallel) nor to continental regions where the rigors of the climate are not checked by the sea. Within these limits, the various varieties can grow in more northerly or southerly areas depending on how early their shoots appear, their temperature requirements during their life cycle* (a need that increases around 45 percent from the beginning to the end of the year), and the time of the year at which they ripen.

The amount of sun also plays a crucial role since it determines plant photosynthesis and hence the quantity of sugar in the vine, and more especially in the grapes: early-fruiting varieties reach maturity after 1,200 hours of sunshine, while later ones require around 1,600. The amount of sun the vines receive is not only dependent on local topography (which way the slopes face, how steep they are, the presence of a hill or mountain nearby), but also on how the vineyard is laid out (the direction of the rows, the space between them, canopy management and so on).

The third, and perhaps most complicated, climatic factor is water. As well as the rainfall required for the vine to survive, other parameters include the soil's* capacity to retain water, the wind, humidity, the dew, as well as the resistance of the rootstock and the vine growth to drought. All of these can radically affect the behavior of a vine in a given climate. DLCDF

▨ Collecting

The motives of great wine collectors vary widely: sheer enthusiasm, speculation, snobbery.... Some, like the American Bipin Desai or the German Hardy Rodenstock, are thoroughbred wine lovers who share their vast collections with other enthusiasts the world over at large-scale tasting events. Others stockpile rare bottles*: today they like to track down new "cult" wines which, though they have not yet proved themselves over time, attract sky-high prices*.

It is obviously absurd to accuse all collectors of being merely label* buffs incapable of judging the wine they possess. Having money in the bank doesn't mean one can't appreciate a Montrachet! The most patient among them know how to

Cellars at Château Lafite-Rothschild, Pauillac, France.

keep wine in the cellar lovingly and to wait until it reaches the peak of perfection before sharing it with a few friends. Nonetheless, it is only human to be a little envious of the Hong Kong collector Henry Tang, with his 40,000 bottles of the finest wines, or of the American Bill Koch, who owns 28,000 bottles, including a Château Lafite 1737 that cost around 100,000 dollars. If, as Scott Fitzgerald had it, "the rich: they're different from the rest of us," it is only, as Hemingway countered at the time, because "they have more money"—and more wine! ER

■ Consumption

The consumer's general tendency is to drink less wine but of better quality. A plethora of wine magazines has been launched on both sides of the Atlantic, indicative of an increased interest in the subject, but the production of the *grand crus* simply cannot meet the demand (see Prices). At the same time, the figures show a gradual reduction in world consumption, which has dropped from 28,574,600,000 liters in 1980, to a 1996 figure of 22,322,500,000—a significant drop of 21 percent over sixteen years.

The top producing nations are still among the highest consumers of wine per head per year: France leads with 60 liters, followed by Italy* (58.05 l), Portugal (53.02 l) and Spain* (37.7 l). The drop in basic consumption has left a wine lake. The strategy adopted by producers today is to expand markets in what are not traditional wine-drinking countries, such as the USA* and China. Among English-speaking countries, the most enthusiastic consumers, Australia and New Zealand, are also producers, though they are followed by the United Kingdom, South Africa, and the predominantly beer-drinking USA. ER

■ Cuisine

Greek and Roman cooks in the ancient world* were already using wine to add savor to their recipes. With oil and brine, boiled with herbs and saffron, flavored with spices, reduced, and sweetened with honey—wine was everywhere. It was used to soften tough meat, to freshen salted meat, and to purify, thicken, and enhance flavors generally.

The Middle Ages* were to take up where antiquity left off, as the marinades, soups, jellies, sauces, cakes, and compotes listed in various medieval recipe books amply display. The Roman tradition for sweet-and-sour persisted: vinegar* and verjuice (juice extracted from unripe grapes preserved in salt or vinegar) both played their part. In the eighteenth century*, wine continued to be an inspiration to bourgeois and regional cuisine. Unsophisticated dishes (fish stews, casseroles, and ragouts) appeared side by side with other, more elegant recipes, such as beef bourguignon, *coq au vin* (chicken in a red wine sauce), lampreys, crawfish, and hare, that called for great wines such as Banyuls, *vin jaune*, Médoc, and Chambertin.

Today, contemporary cuisine, though very health-conscious, has by no means stopped using wine. Its gas-

tronomic advantages have been joined by dietary ones: it reduces the salt and fat uptake, the alcohol evaporates during cooking, while tannins improve digestion (see Health). It is as well, however, not to toss the dregs from some second-rate bottle* into a pan, though neither should the finest vintages* be wasted in a sauce. There are innumerable ways a wine can match a dish, some relying on harmony, others playing with contrast. In doubtful cases, one rarely goes wrong in marrying a local recipe with a wine from the same region. In any case, personal preference rules, and trial and error is all part of the game. Certain hackneyed notions should be cast by the wayside, however: red wines* go very well in fact with certain fish dishes; the majority of cheeses are more in harmony with white wine*; champagne* at dessert is criminal, unless it leans toward the *demi-sec*; and Alsace* Muscat with asparagus is an unbeatable combination. TT

A slice of Comté cheese and a glass of Château-Chalon *vin jaune* from the Jura.

DECANTERS

Decanter.

■ Decanters

To decant or not to decant, that is the question. Should wine be decanted? Is a decanter or a carafe more suitable? Lengthy exposure to air is not as beneficial to wine as people imagine, and many experienced tasters prefer wines served directly after pulling the cork.

Quite apart from the pleasure a fine decanter affords the eye—one preferably in clear glass and funneling out toward the top so as to increase the surface of contact between the air and the wine—decanting is to be recommended above all in the case of wines whose molecules

Annibale Carracci,
Young Boy Drinking,
c. 1582.
Oil on canvas.
Private collection,
New York.

require the "stimulation" a little oxygenation gives. This is true for a number of young, strong, and tannic red wines*, and even for a few whites* (*grand cru* Chablis or Hermitage). The same is true for a few wines that may feel "closed" (i.e. underdeveloped), such as certain Bordeaux* less than ten years old. A little fresh air can breathe life into such sleeping beauties.

Decanting is best reserved for old wines, and sometimes for younger ones that have been bottled without being filtered so as to separate off the sediment, the solid matter deposited by the tannins and anthocyans (coloring compounds) during aging*. Beware: the process can prove something of a rude awakening for certain fragile old wines with a delicate bouquet.

Finally, the widespread practice of opening a bottle an hour or two before drinking to let it "breathe" has practically no effect on the wine. On the other hand, a good wine glass, chosen for its full, tulip-like shape rather than its fancy looks, fulfills the same function as a decanter. ER

44

■ Dionysus

Son of Zeus and the Theban princess Semele, he is the only Greek god born of parents who were not both divine. His ambivalent origins hint at the sacred links that wine forges between earth and the heavens. Born of the fire that ripens the grapes and of the rain that feeds the fields, Dionysus' nature was twofold: cruel, yet also kind. His cult, too, swung wildly between the joyous and heady freedom of the feast and the savage inebriation of the drama. A tragic and idolized divinity, the incarnation of wine and the vine, Dionysus followed the cycles of the plant.

Stumbling across a piece of wood one day, Dionysus placed it inside a bird's bone which he put into a lion's bone and then into the bone of an ass. Planted on the island of Naxos, it grew into the very first vine-plant, since wine first makes men twitter like birds, then gives them the courage of a lion, and finally makes them asinine. The nature of wine too is dual: beneficent and delicious, its subtlety warms the heart, inducing courage and self-confidence. Destructive and merciless in the folly of drunkenness*, however, it destroys the will.

In winter, as the cold descended, Dionysus died an atrocious death, torn to pieces by the Titans. The pitiful stump of vine looked dead, but in the spring, the stubborn plant came back to life, and its return was warmly welcomed. Like Jesus, Dionysus was a symbol of sacrifice and resurrection, of death and rebirth (wine is also identified with Christ—see Eucharist). PÉD

Dionysus on Board Ship. Detail from a black-figure vase, fourth century B.C. Staatliche Antikensammlungen und Glyptothek, Munich.

Disease

In former times, winegrowers most feared hail and frost. In the nineteenth century*, new mortal enemies of the vine made their presence felt. In 1827, it was pyrale, the meal moth. Scalding the vines in winter solved this problem. In 1845, oidium or powdery mildew appeared and was only checked by sulfur treatment.

In 1864, phylloxera raised its ugly head in the Gard region. The larva of this louse, introduced into Europe in cuttings imported from the United States*, destroyed more than two million hectares in a few years. After many trials and tribulations, the only solution was found to be to graft the European vines onto American rootstock that had already proved resistant to the louse. In 1878, the mildew fungus in its turn accompanied the mass importation of American rootstock. The remedy was found to be *bouillie bordelaise* or Bordeaux mixture, based on copper and lime. These intermittent scourges sounded the death knell for many marginally profitable vineyards and resulted in a sea-change in viticulture.

European grape moth, leaf degeneration, yellowing of the vines, eutypiosis…the list is growing, and none of these dangers has been fully eradicated. Another danger lies in the excessive use of chemicals: for a growing proportion of producers* today, hope resides in a "measured response," more respectful of the balance of Nature. The most recent nightmare is a new variety of phylloxera that destroys vines previously thought immune.

A rather different case is provided by *Botrytis cinerea* that causes not only harmful "gray rot," but also beneficent noble rot, which gives great liqueur wines* such as Sauternes. TT

Domaine, Clos and Château

None of these terms in themselves guarantee the origin, and still less the quality, of a given bottle of French wine: they are, in effect, brand names.

In the Middle Ages*, the *clos* (enclosure) was a walled vineyard with a single tenant farmer, which generally belonged to a monastery. By the twelfth century, Cistercian monks in Burgundy had begun to build walls around vines that regularly seemed to give the wines made from them a distinctive character. As well as the Clos de Tart, the Clos du Chapitre and the Clos de Bèze, there was the famous Clos de Vougeot, which, by 1336, had become the largest vineyard in all Burgundy (50 hectares). At the time of the French Revolution*, Church property was confiscated and shared out. Nevertheless, the *clos* still

Vines infected with phylloxera being torn out in the Médoc, France, in the early nineteenth century.

survive and have recently provided the inspiration for some prestigious labels*, such as Clos du Mesnil in Champagne*. The denomination *Château* is of Bordeaux* origin. In 1850, it was already being used by around fifty vineyards, but by 1983 the number had reached more than four thousand. This huge increase was the work of wine-shippers alive to the positive connotations of the word. In France, it designates, in principle, an individual business with its own cellar (*chai*) for making wine, and concerns a wine that is the only one produced by this particular winery. But omissions and exceptions exist: "châteaux" are to be found in many French vineyards and the term (like that of "estate" on US labels) appears on wines made by cooperative wineries. As for the frequent tag *domaine*, it has absolutely no historical or legal meaning.

A wine's image is also conveyed by its name and its label. Today's trend is to personalize wine as far as possible, identification being mistakenly connected in the public mind with some kind of quality guarantee. A growing number of consumers want to relate the wine they drink to a particular estate, *terroir*, producer, or even hillside! Whatever its denomination, however, wine can only be judged in the glass*. TT

47

The annual "Paulée" banquet to celebrate the grape harvest, Meursault. Photograph Henri Cartier-Bresson.

■ Drinking Songs

The grape harvest is hard but convivial work. Muscles groan with the effort, the sun beats down, but the ambience is jovial. For centuries, the grape harvesters have accompanied their work with a song to make the hours pass more quickly. During the French Revolution, the songs shared in the vineyards were a way of stirring up popular feeling against the oppressors, and many of the songs of rebellion and revolt dating from that time are still remembered today, bearing witness to the deep-rooted culture of humble country workers. Early on, these traditional songs were collected by those interested in folk culture: in 1775, a book appeared in London entitled *Buck's Bottle Companion*, "being a complete collection of humorous, bottle and hunting songs, among which are a great variety of originals." The genre naturally gave rise to a fair amount of ribaldry and licentiousness: the poets sang the glories of "wine, women and song," (the name of a waltz by Johann Strauss) and many an immortal melody of Schubert is dedicated to the taste of fine wine, such as "Wein und Liebe" (Wine and Love).

Today, the tradition has not died out: every year, in Pécs, in Hungary, a "Convivial Wine Song Festival" is held to celebrate this fine and ancient genre. TT

■ Drunkenness

Wine makes you drunk—that much has been known since the beginning of history. For thousands of years, being drunk on wine was considered sacred, since, through it, man could reach the gods. The Bible and Christianity, however, both condemn intemperance: a source of joy "when it moveth itself aright," wine "biteth like a serpent and stingeth like an adder" (Prov. XXIII) when abused, leading to debauchery and crime. Drunkennness was indeed a problem, even in monasteries: in the eleventh century, an abbot named Burchard from Worms, in Germany, felt the need to publish a guide entitled *Decretum* setting out punishments for drunken monks, depending on the seriousness of their misdemeanour. In the Renaissance*, however, Bacchus was less demonized, and poets once again sang of creative intoxication. Kings and princes often being heavy drinkers, the Church was forced to compromise. Abuse of alcohol was still condemned, but a taste for good wine was allowed, even if Richard Ames published a work called *Fatal Friendship; or the Drunkard's Misery* in the 1690s. In the eighteenth century*, drunkenness was regarded as a sin more venal than mortal.

By the nineteenth century*, public attitudes to alcohol were changing. Excess acquired a new name in the text *Alcoholismus Chronicus* (1849) by the Swedish doctor, Magnus Huss. The drunk is a social danger; as for women drinkers, they plumbed the depths of social degradation. Temperance Leagues and the like sprang up all over Europe and the New World. For a large proportion of drinkers in Europe, however, wine was not the culprit: tipsiness was still regarded as nothing to be ashamed of, and wine was nothing more than a cheap drink that was a necessity for the working man.

Although the circumstances have changed, the debate still rages today. Alcohol abuse is still a massive killer (on the roads and elsewhere), but, for its supporters, wine remains a source of pleasure and the mark of civilization. Some might contend that when quality—and not quantity—is the rule, it is not the vine that is entirely to blame. TT

The English After Dinner. Plate from *English Scenes Drawn in London by a French Prisoner of War*, c. 1810. Bibliothèque Nationale de France, Paris.

Jean-François de Troy, *Lunching on Oysters*, 1735. Oil on canvas. Musée Condé, Chantilly.

■ Eighteenth Century

In the middle of the seventeenth century, the British aristocracy was on the lookout for new pleasures and had the means to pay for them. In conjunction with technical innovations in bottle-making, this "English thirst" catalyzed what was a revolution in taste. Guyenne "black wines" or "new French clarets" met with phenomenal success: full-bodied and alcohol-rich, they were scarce—and expensive. British importers and French estate owners became more organized. The Graves and Médoc vineyards (see Bordeaux) were drained and replanted. Pruning, selecting, and blending went on apace, and the wine was stored in new casks that were sterilized with sulfur.

Provenance and vintage years* were now put on the labels. Based on price, wine hierarchy has changed little since 1740. In 1787, for instance, Thomas Jefferson drew up his own personal classification*. Top of the bill: Margaux, Latour, Haut-Brion, Lafite. Soon all Europe was to follow this lead. Around 1663, the famous *vin d'Aÿ* was to meet a strange twist of fate across the Channel. Fascinated by the way it would spontaneously sparkle in spring, the English had the novel idea of bottling it with a pinch of sugar so as to make it fizz all the more: thus was champagne* born. Meanwhile, the monk Dom Pérignon tried to rid his wine of the bubbles that were considered vulgar, but eventually came up with the champagne that still bears his name to this day. It was thus only during the fun-loving Regency of Philippe II (1715–1723) that champagne (named after the Champagne region, north-east of Paris) came into its own, earning a reputation as an upmarket and sophisticated wine. TT

■ Eucharist

All through the Old Testament, the symbols of the grapevine and wine are given great significance. Jesus, whose first miracle was to change water into wine at the Wedding at Cana, said: "I am the true vine and my Father is the vine-grower" (John XV, 1). But above all, for Christians, wine, following the episode of the Last Supper, is the very Blood of the Son of God. "And he took the cup, and when he had given thanks, he gave it to them; and they all drank of it. And he said unto them: This is my blood of the New Testament which is shed for many" (Mark, XIV, 23, 24). Another powerful image, often depicted in medieval art, is that of the Mystic Wine-Press, as described by St. Bonaventura: "Christ, crushed against the Cross like a cluster of grapes in the wine-press, has given out a liquid which is a remedy against all our ills." Essential in the celebration of the Eucharist, wine and the vine were cherished by the monks of the Middle Ages*, just as they always had been in the ancient world*. In the twelfth century, however, the Roman Catholic Church, wanting to emphasize the hierarchical superiority of the clergy over the faithful, reserved the wine in the chalice for the priest alone. Only the Churches of the East persisted in taking Communion in both forms. TT

Nardon Penicaud, *Calvary*. Enamel on copper. Musée National du Moyen-âge, Paris.

◼ FERMENTATION: YEAST GETS TO WORK

To transform grape juice into wine, it needs to ferment. The term "alcoholic fermentation" denotes the transformation of sugar contained in the grapes into alcohol (essentially ethyl-alcohol) and carbon dioxide. More or less simultaneously, a whole range of secondary products are formed (glycerol, acids, higher alcohols, esters, and so on), and they too are absolutely crucial to the quality of the wine. This fermentation process occurs either in an entirely natural fashion, by the action of various yeasts present in the grapes, in the air, and in the vats, or else artificially through the addition of dry yeast selected in an oenological* laboratory. To obtain a wine of quality, fermentation must be closely supervised.

Increasingly, vats are installed with temperature-sensitive devices that monitor the rate of fermentation: this can be started or accelerated by using heat, or else slowed down or halted by cooling. Such adjustment is easier in stainless-steel vats than in traditional oak* casks.

The specific component of secondary fermentation, also known as malolactic fermentation, is the action of lactic bacteria that break down malic acid into lactic acid. This occurs for the most part in spring and makes the wines rounder and more stable by diminishing their acidity. It is avoided, however, for some white wines*, such as those from the Rhône valley, in order to preserve their freshness. DLCDF

◼ The French Revolution

By the end of the eighteenth century*, France had a population of some 27 million, the highest in Europe. The court had a thirst for wine, but the winegrowers themselves had to make do with low-quality *piquette* (made from pressed grape skins). The common people thronged to *guinguettes** to drink tax-free. By 1786, shortages, high prices, and altercations with tax gatherers sparked riots first in Lyon, and then in Paris. As well as demands for bread, the people's lists of grievances included appeals for wine. From July 11–13th, 1789, in Paris, rioters set fire to the tax barriers to the city; on the 14th, an unruly crowd stormed the Bastille; on the 23rd July, the populace massacred the regional governor, Bertier de Sauvigny, and ate his heart, minced with wine and alcohol.

The suppression of the shameful taxation system on May 1st, 1791, at last allowed the free movement of wine. Soon everyone wanted his own vine, the symbol of liberty. The English custom of toasting gained ground: red wine* was downed in the name of Liberty and the Nation during collective drinking celebrations. Whereas in Boswell's *Life of Johnson* and other eighteenth-century documents, patriotic (or sometimes

Caffée des Patriotes (detail). Color engraving by S. B. Morret after Jean-Jacques Swebach, c. 1791. Musée Carnavalet, Paris.

Malolactic fermentation, cellars of the Castello di Ama estate, Tuscany.

illegal Jacobite) toasts occur, in post-Revolution texts, when and to whom one made a toast (to King or Queen, or to Whig or Tory) became a political act of some significance.

The period of revolutionary government known as the Directory (1795–99) was a time of greater sobriety: wheat ousted the vine, wine became once more scarce and expensive, and there was a general lack of cash. In 1798, a modified local tax was re-introduced to stop the cities becoming bankrupt. At the same time, the great estates* of the Church and the nobility were confiscated. The situation led to the breaking up of prestigious *crus,* particularly in Burgundy, seriously undermining the quality of its wines. TT

Fortified Wines

Many people treat port and other fortified wines as all-purpose aperitifs. Remarkable wines of this type do exist, however, well worth drinking for their own properties. The common principle in their production is known as "fortifying," in which alcohol is added to the grape must before or during fermentation*. Depending on the amount added, the wine reaches between 15 and 22 degrees of alcohol. According to the moment when the must is fortified, the wine will contain a greater or lesser quantity of residual sugar. *Mistelle* is the name given to fresh must fortified with other than pure alcohol. This occurs in the case of fine *digestifs* such as Cognac or Armagnac, and lesser-known drinks such as Macvin from the Jura* and Ratafia from Burgundy* or from Champagne*. The result marries the fruitiness of grape must (two-thirds) to the complexity of eau-de-vie (one-third). *Vin doux naturel** is produced from a partially fermented must made from grapes from an AOC district, fortified with pure alcohol. The best known are Banyuls, Rivesaltes, Maury, and Muscat. They can have a vintage year*, be bottled rapidly, or alternatively, aged for several years in large barrels. They rarely attain the sophistication of port, however, which is fortified with brandy.

Wines such as sherry, Marsala, Malaga, and Madeira are other examples of delicious fortified wines, which deserve to come back into fashion after some years of neglect. Sherry was formerly one of the most widely made wine styles, and *Sherryana,* published in London in 1886 by one F.W. Cosens, even tells of sherries made in Australia. Madeira's particular flavor came from its transport to the tropics in sea-matured casks: the hot weather made a great change to its taste. Today, the conditions of a long sea voyage are recreated in a process known as "estufa," heating and artificially aging the wine. DLCDF

Pineau des Charentes, Segonzac.

Fraternities

There are hundreds of wine associations, fraternities, commanderies, and brotherhoods today, all over the world. Every year, they celebrate the world of wine, enrolling fellow wine-lovers during joyous festivals where there are flowery speeches and plenty of wine. Many of them hark back to local companies or drinking clubs dating from the Middle Ages* or the early eighteenth century*, but their prime role now is to promote their region and the quality of its wine.

The Chevaliers du Tastevin, the first "modern" *confrérie* and one of the most famous, made its appearance in 1934, right in the middle of a market slump in Burgundy*. Its creation signalled the rebirth of the old seventeenth and eighteenth-century Bacchic guilds which had fallen into oblivion. Today, it has branches in New York, Australia, Hong Kong, and even as far afield as the Bermudas, Senegal and Tahiti—in fact, wherever there are lovers of good wine wishing to perpetuate a fine ancient tradition. TT

Gaul

Unlike the civilised Romans, the Gauls—"barbarous drunkards," as they were lampooned in Greco-Roman writings—drank their wine undiluted, avidly, and without intellectual debate! Starting around 650 B.C., this passion, however, made wealthy men of Etruscan, Greek, and Roman wine shippers. Sailing down the navigable rivers or conveyed by cart from the Rhône* valley as far as Cornwall and Germania, the trade in wine earned these entrepreneurs such large sums

The brotherhood of the Chevaliers du Tastevin at the Château de Clos Vougeot.

Fall, treading the grapes. Fragment of a mosaic from Saint-Romain-en-Gal, early third century. Musée des Antiquités Nationales, Saint-Germain-en-Laye.

of money that it seemed as if local production* did not exist.

Gaul's first vines had been planted by Phoenician colonists near Massalia (today's Marseilles) around 600 B.C., but it was the Roman conquest (the first century B.C.) that really launched the vine-growing economy. Around the southern city of Narbonne, Gaul was carpeted in vines up to the blazing escarpments of Hermitage and Côte-Rôtie to the north, and to the Gaillac region in the west. Two centuries later, the discovery of hardier vine varieties made it possible to extend the vineyards northwards (thanks to Allobrogica, probably the ancestor of Syrah and Mondeuse) and westwards (thanks to Biturica in the Bordeaux* region).

Domitian's edict ordering the vines to be uprooted in A.D. 92, so as to give a helping hand to Roman wines and traders, was only patchily observed, and did not, for example, prevent the creation of the Burgundian vineyards around A.D. 200. In A.D. 280, Probus repealed the edict and the grapevine once more marched out to conquer Gaul. Almost nothing at all is known of the taste of Gaulish wine—except that it met with considerable success, even in Rome. TT

■ Germany

The Romans introduced wine-making on the banks of the Rhine and of the Mosel (see Ancient World). Today, German production* is mainly centered on white wine*, in particular on early-ripening varieties such as Riesling, Sylvaner, and Müller-Thurgau that can produce some fine wines. The best areas are found to the south of the country, bordering the rivers that shelter the vines from the worst of

Hillsides in the Rhine valley, Bacarach, Germany.

the continental climate* and reflect the sunlight onto the vineyards' south-facing slopes. Although the regulations governing the industry were revised in 1971, the division into regions, sub-regions, and vineyards proper remains something of a puzzle. The wines are classified* according to their sugar content (degree of ripeness) at the time of the harvest*. Alcohol levels are generally on the low side, often around 9 or 10 degrees, and it is the acidity that firms up the wine and stabilizes the sugar. Quality fine wines (*mit Predikat*) use grapes harvested in successive pickings. The most renowned are the Trockenbeernauslese (TBA) made of grapes attacked by noble rot, and Eiswein, from a harvest following an early hard frost (12°F or -7°C). Germany exports a good proportion of its production to Great Britain and the United States*, in particular the well-known Liebfraumilch, a low-cost, uncomplicated, and slightly sweet wine.

The great Rieslings from the Mosel valley (as well as from its tributaries, the Saar and Ruwer) and from certain sections of the Rhine valley (the Rheingau), whether dry or liqueur wines*, number among the most famous wines in the world. DLCDF

■ Glasses

The quality of the glasses used for drinking exerts a notable influence on our perceptions of a wine. The ideal wine glass is totally transparent, allowing the color of the wine to be admired, and very thin so it feels good against the lips. Filled about a third full, it should be large enough to allow the bouquet of the wine to develop, with no danger of the contents spilling as the glass is swirled. The stem should be long enough to hold without the fingers covering the bowl of the glass, which not only might leave greasy smudges, but can also have an unwelcome warming effect on the wine.

The superb Venetian glasses of the sixteenth century and most fine glassware produced today fulfill these requirements, though recently a new criterion has emerged. The contemporary vogue for aromas prefers glasses that are tapered at the top (though not so much that it gets in the way of the nose of the drinker!) to prevent the precious nuances of the bouquet from escaping too quickly. One can restrict oneself to one or two well-chosen shapes: fine champagne* is happy enough in a good claret (Bordeaux) glass and a waterglass on the table is often a sign of greater refinement than a collection of gilt-encrusted goblets. Finally, the most beautiful glasses in the world let us down if they are not immaculately clean and bear no trace of the smell of closets or wet dishrags. TT

◼ HARVEST: CHOOSE YOUR MOMENT

Every winegrower knows the crucial importance of timing the grape harvest (vintage) to perfection, and of undertaking it under optimum conditions so as to guarantee the highest possible quality of the raw material required to make a drink that is, in principle, capable of giving the greatest possible tasting pleasure.

The date chosen to begin picking what should be ripe, balanced, healthy grapes is a complicated question, since, in a short space of time, weather conditions can ruin an entire year's work. The calendar of the grape harvest varies depending on the region, variety*, and type of wine envisaged. In general, the period falls some time in September or October in the temperate zones of the northern hemisphere and between February and April in the southern.

Photograph by Martine Franck.

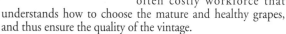

Traditional grape picking is done manually, each bunch being cut separately, or each grape being removed by hand (in the case of Sauternes). The task requires a competent and often costly workforce that understands how to choose the mature and healthy grapes, and thus ensure the quality of the vintage.

The folklore surrounding the exhausting if cheerful work of the traditional vintages has done nothing to stem the soaring popularity of mechanical harvesters since their appearance in the 1960s. Now used in 95 percent of vineyards, they reduce the cost and duration of the grape harvest, though they may entail a drop in the quality of the grapes. ER

◼ Health

According to an ancient saying, wine is both "remedy and poison." In the fifth century B.C., Hippocrates recommended it as an antiseptic and diuretic, to reduce fever and speed recovery. In the second century A.D., Galien listed Greek and Roman wines in his treatise on poison antidotes. Around the eleventh century, the school of medicine at Salerno, in its guidelines on hygiene, noted that wine, drunk in reasonable amounts, could have a positive influence.

Hippocras (mulled wine with sugar and spices) is an age-old remedy for all sorts of ills.

Until the eighteenth century*, the belief was that when wine was drunk, it was transformed into blood in the body. It was given to the sick, women in childbirth, the old, and to everyone in times of epidemic. White wine* was long thought preferable for health, but the physician Fagon went against the general trend in prescribing red Burgundy* to Louis XIV, while Czar Peter I would calm his heartburn with wine from

Cahors. Tokay essenczia was supposed to be able to raise the dead. The idea of wine as an essential food for the laborer became widespread in the nineteenth century* and lasted until around 1950, although the debate on alcoholism, which had initially flared up in 1849, extended to wine in the 1890s. Today, it is generally accepted that certain ingredients of wine, tannins for example, may help guard against cardio-vascular disease by strengthening arterial walls and lowering cholesterol levels, as part of a healthy lifestyle. The message today is—except in the case of medical advice—"drink less, but drink better quality wine." TT

James Ensor, *A Woman Eating Oysters*, 1882. Oil on canvas. Koninklijk Museum voor Schone Kunsten, Antwerp.

Jacques d'Arthois
(1613–1686),
*Wine-merchants
in Flanders.*
Musée Fabre,
Montpellier.

■ Highways and Byways

Wine has come a long way since its early days. It was introduced to Europe by the Phoenicians, although the oldest traces of wine-making are to be found in modern-day Georgia. Moving wine from one place to another was always rather difficult, as cargoes were easily spoilt. Transportation improved significantly in the seventeenth and eighteenth centuries*, however, and thus the majority of wine came to be moved via the new road network—though river and canal transport, which shook up the wine less, were also developing fast. People in the smaller towns drank local wine, while the big cities were supplied on a regional basis. Lyon, for instance, was supplied with Rhône wine by the Rhône barges. Bordeaux was a major trading center as well as producer, reshipping wine by sea abroad or to Paris. Vines grew within Paris too (and do to this day, albeit in small quantities), to supply local needs. Other major trade crossroads were Orleans, Dublin, and London, this last facing somewhat of a crisis when, after the American War of Independence, certain newly free states, such as North Carolina, decided that as from January 1770, no "slaves, wine, nor goods of British manufacture" would enter the colony.

Vines were also transplanted in Australia and South Africa by eager colonists looking for a source of revenue, and although they did not initially flourish, these "New World" producers are now making some of the finest wines in the world. TT

■ Italy

The history of wine is the history of Italy itself, the land the Greeks called Oenotria. With approximately 60 million liters, Italy is the greatest wine producer* in the world by volume, before France, and far ahead of Spain. The climate*, uniformly warm but cooled by the sea air, gives vintages* that are less varied than in France, but has allowed every one of Italy's twenty administrative regions to produce its own wine. Only a few, however, are quality-oriented, with yields scrutinized and the introduction of methods such as temperature control, and aging in oak casks.

Italian classification*, introduced in 1963, has catalogued some 500 wines that range from *Denominazione di Origine Controllata* (DOC, around 15 percent of production) down to more modest country and table wines. Among some 230 appellations, thirteen are *controllata*, where the wine is bottled in its region of origin and is subjected to graded tastings. These wines constitute the cream of Italian wine, but the often bold, if a little rough and ready, *vini da tavola* (table wines) can harbor pleasant surprises.

Piedmont is the cradle of powerful wines such as Barolo and Barbaresco (for laying down), made from the great Nebbiolo grape variety, which have acquired an international reputation in spite of limited production. From the same region, Asti Spumante is the best known of all Italy's sparkling wines.

The second well-known region is Tuscany, whose fine wines are for the most part made from the Sangiovese grape. Chianti is made south of Florence and has been famous at least since the thirteenth century, though in fact its quality is far from uniform. Farther afield one meets with Brunello, Montalcino, and the Vino Nobile di Montepulciano, which are justifiably highly prized today. DLCDF

Bunches of grapes being dried on racks after harvesting. Cellar at Avignonesi, producer of Vino Santo, Tuscany.

■ THE JURA AND SAVOY

The Jura and Savoy regions have acquired quite a reputation in spite of the relatively small scale of their vineyards, around 2,000 hectares each. The former is known for a truly great wine that every wine lover should learn to appreciate: *vin jaune* ("yellow wine"). The second, more prosaically, has emerged thanks to the growing popularity of skiing vacations, and the traditional *fondue* and *raclette* cheese recipes that go with them.

Savoy's vineyard system is indescribably complicated in terms of its appellations. Briefly, it offers light, tangy whites* that mostly ought to be drunk cold, with fairly light cheese-based meals. Demanding wine lovers may also be intrigued by two other wines that can be exceptional, the red Mondeuse (Mondeuse Arbin in particular) and Chignin-Bergeron (made from the Marsanne grape that comes from the Rhône).

The majority of the Jura's vineyards are located in the Revermont region, and is divided into four appellations. The Côtes-du-Jura run from the north to the south of the *département* (administrative district), along the low plateau of the Jura. Exposed to the east, they are sheltered from the harsh climate* of the high plateaus. The Arbois district lies around the wine-growing center of the same name and, like the Côtes-du-Jura, produces reds, rosés*, whites, and *vin jaune*, as well as sparkling wines. The Étoile district is devoted entirely to white wines*, whereas Château-Chalon focuses on *vin jaune.*

White wines* made from Chardonnay can be delicate and rich in minerals, but, when blended* with a typical

Vin de paille and *vin jaune.*

Vineyard at Abymes de Myans, Savoy.

Jura grape, the Savagnin, the wine shows great individuality. *Vin jaune* (known as Château-Chalon when produced in the village of the same name) is made exclusively from Savagnin grapes, and aged in cask for six years. Once bottled in special bottles*, it is almost immortal, and, in France, is a favorite wine for laying down when children are born. The reds are fermented from Poulsard and Trousseau grape varieties and can, when not blended with Pinot noir, give fine and original wines.

Vin de paille, often confused with *vin jaune*, is in fact a true dessert wine* obtained by drying the grapes on a bed of straw (hence the name of "straw wine") for two or three months in an airy loft. This wine can be compared with the very best Hungarian Tokay. DLCDF and PÉD

■ Labels

The label is the wine's personal identity card. Depending on the country of origin, some information is mandatory, some optional. The label, as a minimum requirement, has to mention the wine's geographical origin, the name of the producer and bottler, the net contents of the bottle*, and the degree of alcohol. In the USA, the mentions of wine type, the phrase "contains sulfites," and a government health warning are also obligatory. A vintage* wine will, of course, also display the year it was made, often on a small neck-label. More and more terms are appearing that offer no guarantee as to the quality or otherwise of the contents: in France, *grand vin, cuvée prestige*, and *vieilles vignes*, and also in the USA, "organic wine," "unfiltered wine," "oak-aged," and "reserve." At best, these descriptions may reassure the consumer about the quality of care given to the wine.

There is a thirst for knowledge as well as for wine: the label on the back of the bottle can carry a description of the wine, indicating the weather conditions prevailing at the harvest and its date, the wine-making techniques, and can even make suggestions as to how to serve the wine and which foods to drink it with, etc. Back labels help to inform less expert consumers and novices who want guidance, for whom the obligatory information on the front label is often completely incomprehensible. ER

Right:
Red wine
being racked
from the barrel.

VIN D'ALSACE

APPELLATION ALSACE CONTROLÉE
RIESLING
98 cl
MISE EN BOUTEILLE A LA PROPRIÉTÉ
P. KIRSCHNER Prop.-Viticulteur A 67650 DAMBACH-LA-VILLE France

HANSI

■ LANGUEDOC-ROUSSILLON

Nestling on the Mediterranean shore between Arles and Banyuls, a large number of vineyards in Languedoc-Roussillon date back to the time when Greeks were leaders of the known world (see Ancient World). Spurred by increasing demand in the nineteenth century*, the vineyards slowly descended from the high slopes to reach the plain, and the wines increased in number. With the arrival of the railroad, the region was transformed into a supplier of lost-cost red* "carafe wines," and acquired the unflattering reputation which it suffers from to this day. In fact, especially during the last ten years, Languedoc has been undergoing something of a wine renaissance, and many foreign buyers, amongst them some very well-known figures, now come to stock up in the region on cheap but good wines.

It is true that with around 10 percent of world production*, an exceptional diversity of soil (shale, gravel, calcareous clay, alluvial, etc.) and of grape varieties, reasonable production costs, and relatively liberal regulations, Languedoc-Roussillon has certain

Vines at Périllos, Côtes du Roussillon.

advantages. The reduction in high-yield grape varieties* such as Aramon, and their replacement with higher quality ones such as Syrah, Grenache, Cabernet, and Merlot, as well as Mourvèdre, has been a further factor in these changes. The large amount of land under vine cultivation and the different grape varieties* mean that the region has responded readily to the increased demand for vintage wines* initiated by the emerging wine-producing nations. Finally, the appearance of some first-rate growths has shown that the region can pro-duce great red wines*, and has given renewed hope to growers once tempted to dig up their vines. The Coteaux-du-Languedoc blazed the trail and were followed by Saint-Chinian, Minervois, and Côtes du Roussillon. The still rustic Corbières has some headway to make, and Fitou and Collioure seem set in their ways. In a slightly different realm, sweeter wines (the *vins doux naturels**), which occasionally lack finesse due to excess alcohol and sugar, are having a hard time adapting to the crisis, especially Rivesaltes. DLCDF and PÉD

◼ Liqueur wines

The European denomination, "liqueur wine," is generally reserved for (not necessarily sweet) white wines* containing 2 ounces (50 g) of residual sugar per liter obtained naturally (below that amount they are denominated *vin moelleux*, literally, mellow wine), without chaptalization (adding sugar), or fortifying (see fortified wines*). There are two categories of liqueur wines, those produced with grapes that are left on the vine to shrivel (or dried on racks), and those made from grapes with noble rot.

In the first case, the harvest* takes place late, the grape remains on the vine for a certain length of time after it has ripened. If the weather is fine after the harvest, then the grapes dehydrate and their sugar content becomes concentrated. This is the process that produces Jurançon (see Southwest France), late-harvested Alsace*, as well as Germany's* Eiswein.

In the second case, the grapes are attacked by a microscopic fungus, *Botrytis cinerea*, as the autumn sun disperses the morning mist. In general, not all bunches or parts of a bunch are affected to the same degree, and therefore picking by hand over many weeks is necessary. Noble rot makes the grapes dry out more quickly and starts off a chain reaction, including, notably, the production of glycerol (giving the impression of a "fatter" wine), and of different types of molecule that will eventually impart honey and caramel aromas to the wine. Sauternes, Alsace wines made from selected grapes, and TBAs from Germany* belong to this type.

The quality of a liqueur wine depends on the balance between sugar and alcohol as well as on sufficient acidity to prevent it cloying and becoming heavy. DLCDF

◼ Literature

In all civilizations, wine has inspired writers, be they poets or philosophers, playwrights or novelists, and the bookish wine lover often bumps into fellow drinkers in his reading. From Homer (and his "wine-dark sea") to Shakespeare, from Byron to Charles Baudelaire, the praises of wine have been sung and its color and effects used in imagery. The Bible frequently uses wine imagery, particularly in the Song of Songs: "Let him kiss me with the kisses of his mouth, for your love is more delightful than wine." (Song of Songs 1:2). The great Persian poet, Hafiz (c. 1320–1389) sang the glories of wine and intoxication: "O Saqi, bring around the cup of wine and then offer it to me / For love seemed easy at first, but then grew difficult." Goethe drew inspiration from the poetry of Hafiz to write his collection *West-East Divan*, which reinvents the age-old

Grapes attacked by *Botrytis cinerea,* or noble rot.

poetical language of wine and love.

Though Chaucer mentions wine, in Renaissance* times, it was, of course, Shakespeare who added most to wine literature. As well as Sir Toby Belch's cry for "a cup of canary" in *Twelfth Night*, Shakespeare's Falstaff more reflectively extolled the merits of "sherris-sack": "It ascends me into the brain; dries me there all the foolish and dull and crudy vapours which environ it; makes it apprehensive [receptive], quick, forgetive [inventive]…" (*2 Henry the Fourth*, IV, 4). Other English-speaking literary lovers of wine included the moody Tobias Smollett, Swift ("less frugal of his wine than of his meat,") Johnson, Lord Byron (for whom hock, soda-water and biscuit was a hangover remedy), the over-indulgent Sheridan, and Thackeray, Dickens, and Evelyn Waugh—a true connoisseur. It is interesting to note that hard-drinking American writers, from Lowry via Hemingway to Bukowski, tend to go for beer and/or spirits. Eschewing Bacchic excesses, the French writer Colette captures to perfection the growth of the vine-plant and its transformation into "velvet" and "flame," and, in her autobiographies, evokes the subtlest perceptions without resorting to "technical" tasting* terms.TT

Étienne Jeaurat (1699–1789), *The Poet Piron at Table with his Friends Vadé and Collé.* Oil on canvas. Musée du Louvre, Paris.

"Think not wine against all good verse offends,
The Muse and Bacchus have always been friends,
Nor Phoebus' blushes sometimes be found,
With ivy, rather than with laurel, crown'd.
The Nine themselves oftimes have join'd the song,
And revels of the Bacchanalian throng;
[…] What in brief numbers sung Anacreon's muse?
Wine & the rose that sparkling wine bedews."

William Cowper, *Elegy III*

69

■ LOIRE VALLEY

A cradle of the Renaissance*, the Loire is a region with enduring cultural, gastronomic, and wine-making traditions. From Nantes to Nevers, past Anjou and Touraine, the great river Loire waters the "garden of France" and provides the sole meandering link between the vineyards of the region, that are of singular variety. The result is a highly diverse range of wines: reds* and whites*, dry and sweeter wines for early drinking, and wines for keeping. Moving down the river to the sea, one first meets Muscadet, a nervy wine made from the Burgundy* Melon grape, that here develops its own particular character thanks to the conjunction of sedimentary rocks and a steady oceanic climate*. With its often steep slopes and shale soil, Anjou produces reds, dry and sweeter whites, as well as dry and, more exotically, sweet rosés*. Primarily, however, the region makes renowned sweet wines such as Coteaux du Layon, Quarts-de-Chaume, and Bonnezeaux. When they have been made following the time-honored rules—late-vintage, sorting, no chaptalization—they become

Château and vineyard at Chinon.

richer as they age, due to the acidity of the Chenin grape. The prolific vines of the districts around Saumur and Tours toil on the chalk of the tufa to produce, from the same Cabernet franc as in Bordeaux, plain-speaking red wines* that are fresh and fruity, such as Champigny and Bourgueil, or more tannic, meaty specimens, like Chinon. Tannic wines are today in favor thanks to scientific research showing that in moderation, they are beneficial to health. The subtler Vouvray and Montlouis, that go so well with the traditional meats and patés of the region, release the flower scents of the Loire's Chenin in dry, *demi-sec*, sweet, or sparkling versions.

Towards the east, almost in the center of France, the climate becomes continental. Around Sancerre and Pouilly-sur-Loire, wine-growers work with Sauvignon, a troublesome grape variety, difficult to manage, but the undisputed master of white wines: lively, with a complex, delicate aroma when the grape is ripe (and the yield monitored), these wines should be drunk while fresh, to taste the fruity flavor. PÉD

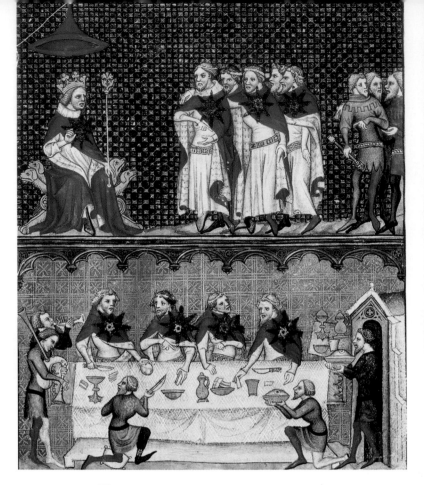

Knights of the Star dining. Miniature taken from *Les Grandes Chroniques de France,* c. 1356. Bibliothèque Nationale de France, Paris.

■ The Middle Ages

Having escaped the invasions of the "Barbarians," the vine survived thanks to the Church. Numerous bishops entered the annals of wine-growing, and every monastery possessed its own *clos* or walled vineyard (see Domaine). Wine was needed for Communion (see Eucharist), for the monks themselves and their patients, and still more for visitors, as well as to ensure revenue for the community. So it was that the vine flourished—especially around Paris and in the Loire valley*—to the extent that references to religious communities still abound in wine names. In the twelfth century, the Cistercians took up where the Benedictines left off and began working in Burgundy*,

Languedoc*, and Béarn. They were also the first to grasp the idea of the *terroir*.

In the fourteenth century, the finest wines were made from Pinot fromenteau (gray) and Noirien (black) varieties. Chaucer's aged knight, taking a younger bride in the *Merchant's Tale,* drinks "vernage" (Tuscan vernaccia), "claree" (*clairet*—the ancestor of the word claret), and "hippocras" (spice-wine). Indeed the latter (with "gynger, synamon and graynes, sugour and tur[n]esoll [sunflower seeds]") was universal in England. At the beginning and end of banquets, after a ceremony, the pass-cup or wassail-bowl was passed from person to person. The meal was rounded off with highly prized dessert wines, such as Malvoisie

72

(Malmsey), or Muscat from the Mediterranean. In 1478, King Richard III is said to have had the Duke of Clarence drowned in a butt of malmsey, a death befitting his aristocratic status.

Until the sixteenth century (see Renaissance), northern wines predominated in France, either whites* or light *clairets*. Trodden by foot, they were fermented in barrels, fined with honey or egg-white, racked, and topped up to compensate for evaporation. They spoiled all too easily, and to prevent this, winemakers turned to remedies common in the ancient world*: fennel seeds, oak ash, or gall-nuts.

The people drank, in the main, unhealthy water, and a vinegary beverage fermented with the remains of the pressed grapes. In towns, demand exceeded supply and unscrupulous fraudsters watered the wine. The luckiest people owned a few vines and drank their own produce. However it was made, wine always had to be drunk young, since by the following summer it would be vinegary. TT

■ Mythology

The theme of a drink—offered by the gods or purloined by man—that confers immortality is to be found in any number of ancient religions and myths. The "blood of the vine" is closely linked to hopes of resurrection into a better world, while the legendary Tree of Life is often depicted as a grapevine. In the Babylonian epic, *Gilgamesh* (1800 B.C.), the eponymous hero searching for immortality reaches the Kingdom of the Sun and comes upon a miraculous vine whose wine would realize his dream, but he is not permitted to drink it. At Nineveh, the goddess Ishtar was known as the "Mother Vine." In Egypt, certain vines were called the "sweat" of the sun-god Re, or the "tears" of Horus, son of Isis and Osiris. The vine was above all associated with the latter, god of the plant world and the after-life. The myth of Osiris is very close to that of Dionysus*, and the two divinities, first torn apart and then reborn, inevitably recall the figure of Christ (see Eucharist). The myth of Orpheus, a relative of Dionysus, torn to pieces by wine-crazed Maenads, is in turn associated with the land of the dead. He was the inspiration for Orphism, an initiatory religion that believed in the immortality of the soul and whose disciples commonly drank the blood of the god in the form of wine. It is also interesting to note that wine appears at the conclusion of all stories of the Flood or the Ark, whether in the case of Noah, or Orestes (the survivor from primitive humanity spared by Zeus) or Jamshid, a Persian king who led the animals into an enclosure to save them, and by chance discovered the effects of wine thanks to a jar of grapes left behind in a corner of his palace. TT

Guardian spirit offering a libation to a sacred tree. Stone bas-relief from the Royal Palace at Nimrud (Iraq), ninth century B.C. British Museum, London.

◼ Nineteenth Century

During the nineteenth century, farmers and workers in wine-growing countries were well used to drinking wine, while the wine market overall was expanding. In response to the demand, vines were planted, often in inappropriate places. High-yield varieties and hybrids were the most popular and use of fertilizer became commonplace. Unscrupulous wine merchants used blueberries, caramel, or infusions of mignonette (a flower used for dye) to give color and perfume to the pale beverages that, like cheap imported wine from Spain*, Italy* or Algeria, made their fortune.

Fine wines for the upper classes, however, were becoming increasingly diverse, and knowing what and how to drink became a sign of good breeding. In 1855, the classification* based on the price* of the Bordeaux wines presented at the Paris World Fair gave official sanction to a hierarchy that had been taking shape since 1740. In what was a scientific age, grape varieties were studied, the density of the must measured, and the temperature of wine-vats was taken. Having already made the role of yeast in the process known, in 1865, Louis Pasteur managed to stem the fermentation* of harmful bacteria by heating the mixture. At the end of the century, Hermann Müller-Thurgau demonstrated the effectiveness of sulfur treatment.

In spite of the pests and diseases* that would periodically plague it, the vine's expansion continued apace until the 1870s, when the ravages of phylloxera wiped out vineyards all over Europe, and they had to be replanted from scratch. The most renowned regions, such as Bordeaux*, Burgundy*, and Champagne* replanted their vineyards with grafted vines, and were soon back on their feet. On the other hand, the vine disappeared from less popular regions such as Brittany, Normandy, and Picardy in France. As a measure of the disaster, in 1893, France had lost a third of its vineyards. That year, the harvest was phenomenal, paving the way for a slump in the market that led to the 1907 crash. TT

◼ Oak

The use of oak barrels in the maturing, storing, and transporting of wine is an age-old practice that at one point was more or less abandoned in favor of inert and microbiologically clean materials (stainless-steel, concrete, or plastic vats). The last fifteen years, however, have experienced a revival in storing and maturing wine in wooden vats and barrels.

Research has demonstrated that the role of oak is not limited to its undeniable effect on the wine's aroma. It is a surprising material which is at once almost impermeable yet relatively porous. Various phenomena, first among them a carefully controlled oxygenation (the gas penetrates in infinitesimal, but regular, amounts) make a wooden barrel into a container capable of modifying the structure, composition, and quality of a wine. Of course, there is also the excessive use of new wood to enhance a fruity or lightly structured wine.

Considerable expertise is required to adapt maturing in cask to the wine's origin (from a

more or less prestigious *terroir**) and to the characteristics of the vintage* (an ordinary, or outstanding year). The origin of the wood, the amount of heat the cooper applies to shape it, and the proportion of new casks, will each have an effect.

Each type of timber has specific characteristics that impart a particular flavor and aroma to the wine. Cooperage is not, as some might think, a dying art: many training courses and apprenticeships are available in this ancient craft. DLCDF

Numbered barrelstaves before being bound with metal hoops. Seguin-Moreau Cooperage, Cognac.

◼ OENOLOGY: THE SCIENCE OF WINE

Wine science (from the Greek *oinos*, "wine," and *logos*, "science") has brought immense progress in the areas of wine quality, generally by bringing with it technical improvements in viticulture, vinification*, and winemaking*. Oenologists play an important role as consultants to winemakers who lack sufficient knowledge to master the whole complicated process necessary to produce fine wine. The profession acquired its accreditation in Bordeaux*, through the work of Jean Ribéreau-Gayon, Émile Peynaud, and a whole generation of wine scientists who trained at the *Institut d'Oenologie*. The increasing authority of wine scientists today has become the subject of some debate. The influence of some itinerant oenologists (known in the New World as "flying winemakers"), and their search for a so-called "international" style of an opulent, woody wine supposed to delight critics, is regularly condemned. Michel Rolland, the most influential of all contemporary oenologists (he acts as consultant for more that sixty *domaines** in Bordeaux

and for many estates the world over) is often criticized for having imposed a style that blurs the character of the *terroir**. Though he rejects the accusation, he does express regret over some past excesses. Nevertheless, his work remains a shining example of a search for quality that emphasizes the importance of maximum ripeness and of reducing yield. Modern oenology can help optimize or even transcend the *terroir* by improving the quality of the grapes through better vineyard management and through the elimination of technical shortcomings that can mask the true character of a wine. ER

Michel Rolland.

◼ Opening Wine and Serving Temperature

The keyword for a good wine is balance: balance in respect of the fruit, acidity, alcohol, tannins, etc. The ideal temperature and exposure to air create the conditions that allow the wine's components to be expressed in harmony. Serving temperature is critical. Too cold, and the aroma is locked in; too warm, and acidity or alcohol predominate, throwing the wine out of balance, and making it sour and upset. The classic requirements are these: between 46 and 40°F (8–10°C) for whites* and rosés*, but between 54 and 57°F (12–14°C) for certain truly fine whites; 51–54°F (11–12°C) for light, supple, or fruity reds* with low tannin content; 57–60°F (14–16°C) for Rhône and Burgundy wines, or 60–64°F (16–18°C) for Bordeaux.

Recommendations about letting wine breathe also depend on its character and intensity. The common practice of opening the bottle* some time before drinking has almost no aerating effect since the amount of wine that comes into contact with the air is nominal. For supple or fruity wines, with a marked vintage bouquet, opening the bottle shortly before pouring is normally sufficient.

Decanting may be beneficial for reds, and even for whites that cannot develop in the constricted space of the bottle. It may even be necessary for wines with quite a lot of sediment, though it should be done with great care and at the last minute for very old wines, so as not to damage their fragile bouquet. ER

Origins

The wild vine, a plant blessed with astonishing powers of adaptation, has existed for over two million years.

The abiding question is, when and where was wine first produced? Most experts point to the southern Caucasus at around 7,000 years B.C., the telltale clues being the finds in Georgia of pips from the cultivated grape (*Vitis vinifera sativa*) as well as of a large amphora (*kwevri*) decorated with the motif of a bunch of grapes dating from the sixth millennium B.C. and now conserved in the museum at Tbilisi.

It is in jars like this one, buried up to their necks and sealed with a wooden stopper, that Georgian peasants have been vinifying their wine since time immemorial. After treading, the grapes are poured into a hollowed-out tree-trunk and left to ferment until the following spring. The wine is then transferred into a *kwevri* that is buried in the cool soil to conserve it.

The oldest written and illustrative sources come from Mesopotamia and the valley of the Nile, and go back to around 2,500 years B.C. They reveal the existence of a highly organized—and hence scarcely recent—culture of vine-growing. A few centuries later, Egyptian mummies were being laid out beneath vaulted galleries painted with clusters of fine, black grapes in preparation for the eternal vine harvest. Amphorae recovered from Tutankhamun's tomb indicate the vintage*, the vineyard, and even the name of the "cellarmaster." The vines of the Nile valley are no doubt the ancestors of our present-day red wine* vineyards. From the Near East and Persia, *Vitis vinifera sativa* made its way to India and China, but it was from the west, thanks to the Phoenician mariners who took it to Crete, that it later set out to conquer the world. TT

Valley of the Nobles, Thebes. Tomb of Sennefer, Amenophis II's general, Eighteenth Dynasty.

◼ Organic Wine

Intensive agriculture considers the soil* as a support, there simply to further the plant's development. The latter is fed with all the chemicals it needs and systematically sprayed to eliminate pests and disease*. Excesses in this area have had harmful effects on health, and have led to a more prudent approach to using chemicals and even to new and entirely different ways of thinking.

Organic agriculture treats the soil as an entity that contains various forms of plant and animal life whose balance must be preserved. In European Union countries, the use of fertilizer and synthetic pesticides is prohibited on such farms. In the wake of principles such as these, numerous more or less scientifically based methods have arisen. The most famous is so-called bio-dynamic agriculture, which uses ecological techniques in accordance with a theoretical system that attempts to take into account the "cosmic influences" affecting the life-giving qualities of the soil. Despite the more weird and wonderful features of bio-dynamics, the quality of the wines made by major wine-makers who have been converted to its methods is enough to make one think long and hard about what is a wholly new approach to wine-growing. DLCDF

◼ Paintings

From time immemorial, wine and art have been linked. All the arts praise the intoxicating virtues of a drink that has pride of place at any celebration worthy of the name. Nothing is too good for a beautiful wine as it is poured into cut glass goblets. Wine joins men together in that all too rare moment when they can wish each other "good health." Essentially divine and sacred, it joins souls in brotherhood. Early depictions of the inspirational power of the vine have been found in Egyptian tombs and in Roman mosaics. The sixteenth-century painter Giuseppe Arcimboldo went so far as to depict the male figure of Autumn in the guise of wine, so closely are the two associated. Full of nervous energy in their youth, both man and wine blossom, attaining a precarious balance before drying up and crumbling as time takes its toll. Great artists such as Goya, Renoir, and

"Bio-dynamic" viticulture, Domaine Huet, Vouvray, France.

J. M. W. Turner have all paid homage to the vine and the vintage* as living symbols of the generosity of Nature. Johannes Vermeer painted men and women enjoying a glass of wine as a prelude to seduction. The nineteenth-century* artist, Jean-François Millet, in a more realist vein, painted the strenuous efforts of the cooper.

Wine only reveals its secrets when it has emerged from the obscurity of the cellar and is on the table. Its colors shimmer in many a meditative still life: in seventeenth-century works shot through with Christian morality, wine stands for the vanity of pleasure, and for the transitory nature of human entertainments: for this reason a glass of wine features in many *memento mori* paintings.

Other artists of the same period, such as Frans Hals and Adriaen Brouwer, turned their hand to drinking scenes. An elbow is raised, the cup comes to rest on the lip, the wine is imbibed. Sharing their pleasure or sipping alone, reeling in drunkenness*, or consoling an unfathomable sadness, drinkers throughout history have grown into a single family, bound together by art. The eighteenth century* was to bring wisdom and balance to wine: the brush of Jean-Baptiste Chardin imbues it with a tranquil majesty, and the honest pleasure afforded by drinking is accepted without any reservation. As art developed, wine and its attributes became just one of the elements that impart visual balance to a composition: between two card-players intent on their hands, the bottle is transformed by Cézanne into a silent witness— as if forgetful of the fact that, for the most part, wine loosens tongues and leads to joyful feasting. PÉD

Paul Cézanne,
The Card Players,
1890–95.
Oil on
canvas. Musée
d'Orsay, Paris.

■ PRICES: Ever Upwards, Ever Onwards!

What price should you pay for a five-star bottle of wine? The constant rise in prices for Bordeaux* (even new vintages break records) is of concern for all wine buyers. For the serious wine lover whose pockets are not bottomless, buying good wine has become something of a challenge. It is not worth counting on the recent financial turmoil in the Asian economies to calm an overheated market in the near future: the worldwide demand for fine wines still outstrips supply. The merely average quality of the 1997 vintage, for example, barely slowed the demand for Bordeaux that has been gaining speed since 1995 (with a slight readjustment in 1998). The desire to possess a bottle of vintage "2000" also caused a jump in prices, no matter what the intrinsic quality of the wine. This highly charged atmosphere is characterized by stratospheric prices that are sometimes unjustified. At some much-hyped auctions (such as the collections of Maxim's restaurant, or of Andrew Lloyd Webber in 1997), a varnish of glamor tripled the purely market value of the wine concerned. A Colgin Cabernet-Sauvignon 1994, a wine marketed at less than 100 dollars in 1997, was sold not so long ago for well over $1,000 by Christie's, the auctioneers, in Los Angeles. With no historic pedigree, such wines have yet not proved their aging capacity, and are merely a "cult" product whose main merit lies in their rarity. ER

Photograph,
Gilles Peress.

Production

The amount of land in the world cultivated with vines continued to expand until 1980 to reach around 10,213,000 hectares.

Since then, the arable land devoted to viticulture has fallen, mainly due to vines being plowed up in the countries of the ex-USSR and the European Union, which has encouraged a move away from wine production.

Nonetheless, expansion is still underway in South America*, the USA and China. The latest available figures put the global vineyard at some 7,799,000 hectares.

As to the global production of wine, it has dropped from 27,053,100,000 liters in 1996, to 26,145,900,000 in 1997 and finally to only 25,877,600,000 in 1998, a drop of 4.3 percent over only three years.

A recent upsurge in wine production has not, however, been mirrored by increases in consumption*. In fact, this was on a more or less continuous downward spiral between 1980 and 2000, resulting in a huge wine surplus, especially in Europe, where set-aside has at times been actively promoted by the European Union. ER

■ PROVENCE AND CORSICA

Olive trees, wheat fields, and vineyards make up the three-some of Mediterranean agriculture. Growing wheat has often been a losing battle, but both olive and vine cultivation have met with more success. Provence probably possesses the oldest of all French vineyards, since the vine was introduced in the sixth century B.C. by the Phoenicians or the Phocaeans (see Ancient World). Provence contains three vast vineyards, dedicated essentially to producing rosé*: Coteaux-d'Aix-en-Provence, Coteaux-Varois, and Côtes-de-Provence. There are also four smaller areas: Palette, Cassis, Bandol, and Bellet.

Although the rosés are only really palatable, chilled, in the heat of summer, they are now increasingly well made, fruity, and fresh, and losing their "acid bon-bon" aroma. The most common grape varieties*, which also provide lesser-known reds*, are Grenache (for body), Mourvèdre (for structure), and Cinsault (for finesse). Rhône Syrah and Bordeaux Cabernet sauvignon also play a role in the more venturesome blends*.

Vineyard at Balagne, Corsica.

As for white*, three appellations are justly renowned: Cassis, that produces a wine from Marsanne, Ugni blanc, and Clairette, an ideal accompaniment to seafood (bouillabaisse in particular); Bellet, near Nice; and Palette (just outside Aix), that produce some rare wines made from, respectively, the Rolle and Clairette varieties.

The reds are superbly represented by the Bandol vineyards that flourish on terraces rising up between the sea and the pinewoods around Toulon. Structured by the austerity of the dominant Mourvèdre, and magnificent with game and meaty casseroles, it is one of the few wines in the Midi that achieves finesse with age.

As for Corsica, with its mountainous and varied landscape, its little-known white and red wines* are produced on the coast. Made from local varieties—such as the Sciacarello and Nielluccio for reds, and the Vermentino for whites—they go well with Mediterranean cuisine* and with Corsica's justly celebrated goats' cheese. DLCDF and PÉD

◾ PRUNING
Controlling Yields

The natural inclination of a vine-plant is to become a climber, stretching out interminably and developing in a haphazard manner with tiny little fruit scarcely fit to eat. To obtain grapes that can be made into a decent wine, the winegrower has to curb the plant's natural growth (see Vine Life Cycle) and control the amount of nutrition it receives so as to split its potential for growth between producing fruit (and hence a sufficiently ripe harvest) and enhancing the vigor of the plant (foliage and branch growth, building up reserves for the subsequent year, etc.).

Pruning a vine.

Pruning methods are generally dictated by regulations (except in newly emerged wine-producing countries) or by local usage. In *Guyot* vine cane-training the "wooden" cordon is pruned after every vintage, and a new fresh spur is allowed to grow; *Cordon de Royat* is based on a "cane," or long-standing solid, lignified branch. Numerous variations exist according to the desired yield, or in order to adapt to mechanized picking (vintaging)* methods.

"Dry" winter pruning is the pivot around which the working year revolves, and—since maximizing production is no longer the aim—it is designed to enhance the quality of the wine to come.

After the harvest comes the season for plowing and for fertilizing. At the onset of spring, weeds have to be eradicated, the young branches protected against parasites, and excess new shoots removed; in summer, the branches have to be attached to the stakes, which have to be secured, and this is followed by the removal of excess grapes. DLCDF

◾ Purchase

Once you have settled on a buying strategy—depending on how and how often you drink wine, and on the cellar at your disposal (if any)—you are faced with a raft of options as to acquiring wine. Your local wine merchant is the nearest solution, of course, though the early 1990s recession forced many of the independent stores in Britain and the USA to operate through mail order. It is advisable to establish a relationship of trust with him or her since a good wine merchant is not only a link between you and the producer, but is a person fired with a passion for what they do, who, through a hand-picked selection of wines, can stimulate and broaden your interest.

The wine merchants' main competitors today are supermarkets, hypermarkets, and in the UK, the larger affiliated mail-order companies and clubs. Supermarkets have recently been busy improving the conditions in which they keep and present fine wines, in order to reassure the increasingly wine-conscious consumer initially drawn by their eye-catching prices* even for quality growths.

Though the anonymity of large retail outlets is regrettable, it is a fact that over 70 percent of consumers do their shopping in such stores and, in France, 45 percent of all Bordeaux is sold there.

If you prefer older vintages, certain mail-order wine catalogs offer a range. Wine auctions also have their advantages, though one should keep a tight rein on one's budget and remain vigilant as to the state and provenance of all bottles* purchased.

It is preferable, if not vital, to taste a wine before buying. Wine tourism* also can allow one to "place" the wine in the area in which it grows and even to meet the people who have made it. One should beware, however, of getting carried away and indulging in impulse buying. When traveling through the Bordeaux region it should be remembered that the majority of the *grands crus classés* ("classified great growths") are not on sale to the general public at the estates. ER

◼ RED WINE: THE MUST IS EVERYTHING

Most red grapes have white flesh; it is the skin pigment that colors the wine. The essential characteristic of red wine-making is the practice of leaving the grape juice in contact with the skins so as to extract the color during fermentation* and sometimes longer. The methods used, however, vary depending on the region, the vineyard, and even the winegrower. Once at the winery, the grapes are weighed and the weights noted. They are then sorted, if this has not already been done during the harvesting, or if the quality of the grapes makes it necessary (especially if they have suffered from gray rot).

The grapes, more or less de-stemmed, and lightly crushed, are put into vats and eventually treated with sulfur (sulfur is antioxidant and antiseptic). Compressed under their own weight, the grapes form into must, a mixture of juice, pulp (flesh), and skins, that gradually begins to ferment. Various methods, depending on the grape varieties and the state of the harvest, are used to encourage the release of the coloring substances as well as of tannins: cold pressing, either prior to or after fermentation; immersion of the skin and pulp floating on the surface by pressing it back into the juice using poles; or by spraying it with juice pumped up from the bottom of the vat.

When fermentation is complete, the free-run wine runs out, the skins and pulp are removed from the vat, and the press-wine is extracted under pressure. The free-run and the press wine are then wholly or partially blended* depending on the growths concerned, before being transferred into vats or casks. Then the wine-making* begins. DLCDF

Reference Books

Cato the Censor, Pliny the Elder (in sections of his *Natural History*) and Lucius Columella (*De Re Rustica*) are a rich source of material concerning Roman wine-growing up to the first century B.C. All three refer back to Mago and his collection of Canaanite and Phoenician agricultural traditions, which had been taken up by the Carthaginians by 500 B.C.

The chief reference book of the Middle Ages* was an adaptation of classical sources by Piero di Crescenzia, the *Liber Commodorum Ruralium* (1303). From the Renaissance*, we can cite the *Vinetum* by the physician Charles Estienne. In 1600, Olivier de Serres' *Théâtre d'agriculture* is a model of acuity to which we owe the famous definition: "air, soil, and the vine are the foundations of a vineyard." An early medical treatment of the question of wine is to be found in Dr. Shaw's *The Juice of the Grape*, dating from 1724. He believed wine cured everything from smallpox to gout.

Study of ways to improve vines began in earnest in the eighteenth century*, with the invention of the science of ampelography, or the study of grape varieties. The definitive work on the subject appeared in 1855: Odart's *Ampélographie universelle*. The nineteenth century* provides many such fundamental textbooks. In 1816, André Julien published the impressive *Topographie de tous les vignobles connus* ("Topography of all known vineyards") in which he classified wines from five continents. In 1866 Louis Pasteur published research on his fundamental discoveries on the role of yeast in fermentation. Not all wine reference books were French, however: Alexander Henderson of London published a *History of Ancient and Modern Wines* in 1824, and James Busby published Australia's first wine book, *A Treatise on the Culture of the Vine and the Art of Making Wine*, in 1825. TT

■ Renaissance

During the Renaissance, Bacchus (see Dionysus) made a return to Western culture—first in Italy, then in France—and the god of liberating drunkenness* inspired his fair share of great art, from Shakespeare to the paintings of Giuseppe Archimboldo.

At this time the number of small farmers was increasing, and vines were planted in many different regions. Around 1550, reference books* on wine-making multiplied, and wines began to diversify, each region and each vineyard developing its own unique character. Contemporary French vocabulary* dealing with wine is revealing in the light of this: it had twelve words for acidity and five for smell, of which three were pejorative, indicating the quality of the wine available at the time. In an attempt to improve the quality of their produce, vintners turned their attention increasingly to aging*, and wine became more drinkable in consequence. Oak* became the norm for cooperage, and glassmaking developed, though the fragility of the straw-wrapped bottles* meant they were served only at table. White wines* remained more important in northern

climes. The most popular grape variety was Pinot fromenteau (see Middle Ages). In high society, wines were drunk *à l'italienne*, that is mixed with snow or ice. The majority was dry, though sweeter Muscat and Malvoisie (Malmsey) lost nothing of their prestige (see Vins Doux). Still much in demand were medieval *clairets*, which were essentially a mix of white and black grapes, where the must stayed for one day in the vat after a rough treading without being pressed. The free-run wine was often drained off during fermentation*, the remainder ending up under the press, giving wines known as *vermeil* ("vermilion," i.e. red). In Southwest France*, winemakers experimented with longer periods in the vat, resulting in "black" wines with a higher tannin content which made them more robust. TT

Jean de Gourmont, *Descent into the Cellar*, 1537. Oil on panel. Städelsches Kunstinstitut, Frankfurt.

■ RHÔNE VALLEY

Planted in Roman times (see Ancient World), the vineyards on the banks of the Rhône River running from Vienne in the north to Avignon in the south have made the valley the second most important wine-producing area in the whole of France. Its wine was long associated with Beaujolais*, and, like its counterpart, is considered to be an easy-going, companionable quaffing wine. In fact, its most prestigious growths can hold their own against Bordeaux* and Burgundy*. The northern sector, essentially dominated by Syrah, contains the appellations most in vogue today: Côte-Rôtie, Hermitage, and Cornas. The red wines* produced on the steep slopes of the river valley are rich and full-bodied, and should be laid down for at least five years; those from *terroirs* in Crozes-Hermitage and Saint-Joseph are more supple but just as fruity. The white *viognier* variety—which is often a permitted top-up for reds—shows its individual flavor in Condrieu.

Vineyard at Tain-l'Hermitage.

The Grenache variety takes over in the southern zone, in particular at Châteauneuf-du-Pape and Gigondas. But the very diversity of the reds derives from the skilful blending* of numerous varieties, such as Grenache itself, Syrah, Mourvèdre, Carignan, Cinsault, and others (up to thirteen varieties in the case of Châteauneuf-du-Pape). It is above all the dry, warm climate* swept by the mistral wind, and to a lesser degree, the abundance of granite, that unifies a vast wine-growing region that covers the various regional and communal appellations of the Côtes-du-Rhône (Cairanne, Chusclan, Rasteau, and so on). The whites produced from Grenache blanc, Clairette, Bourboulenc, Marsanne, and Roussanne are sometimes less interesting, but have both body and freshness when the wine has been well made. The white Hermitages, rather austere when young, can become great wines when given time. DLCDF and PÉD

■ ROSÉ: NO MIXING IT

There is no strict, oenological* or statuary definition of rosé. In fact, there are only two methods of vinification*, red* and white*, and rosé is made according to one or the other. It is more often made totally or partially from the free-run wine of a red during pressing; the moment chosen to drain off the juice from the vat is the crucial factor in determining the color of the rosé. The longer it remains on its lees (anything from a few hours to half a day), and hence is in contact with the red pigments in the skins, the deeper the color and more tannic the wine. Later, the juice is put into vats and follows the same process of fermentation* as a white. It is also possible to make red grapes into white wine by not allowing the juice to stay in contact with the grape skins: after crushing, the (white) free-run wine is taken off and the remainder lightly pressed to obtain a faintly colored press-wine. The blending* of these two wines (a very pale rosé, sometimes known as *vin gris*, "gray") is left to settle and then to ferment in the same way as a white, generally at a low temperature to keep its freshness.

Pink champagne is exceptional in that it is often made from a mixture of white* and red wines*. Poulsard, a typical Jura* variety* whose skin and juice are both pink, is another special case: though made like a red wine, it is invariably tinted a charming delicate pink. DLCDF

■ SOIL

The soil is often considered as the most characteristic component of *terroir**. It can neither be exported nor copied, and remains bound to its region of origin. Its influence on the vine is so closely linked to the climate*, to the vineyard's exposure to the sun, and even to human intervention (such as to the choice of rootstock and variety*, or to how the vine is cultivated, etc.) that for all practical purposes there is no such thing as "ideal" vine-growing soil. However, certain soils, such as those on rich and fertile plains, do not provide suitable soil for the grape.

Poorly drained, rather clayey soils, that retain water and have a tendency to become damp and cold, are to be avoided in northern climes, though they may be suitable in regions inclined to drought. On the other hand, gravelly soils, well drained and without much clay, and hence warmer, are well adapted to the climate of France, for example, though not necessarily to every variety of vine: such conditions may be ideal for late-fruiting Cabernet sauvignon, but Merlot, an earlier-fruiting variety, risks ripening too quickly. In fact, a better wine is obtained when the soil and climate slow down the maturing of the grape.

Another factor to be considered is the bedrock located a few centimeters or even meters below the soil proper, which is created by erosion of this rock. An extremely dry soil can be perfectly suitable for vines as long as their roots manage to reach through the cracks in the rock to draw up moisture. In any case, a minimum of clay and humus is a prerequisite in the upper layer of the soil (the arable subsoil) so that the roots can reach the nutrients necessary for the development of the vine, in particular nitrogen, phosphorous, and potassium (the three basic elements of fertilizer, which is often added in excessive quantities). DLCDF

Sommelier

The noble calling of the sommelier (or wine-waiter) has been regaining its former prestige in recent years, as demonstrated by the success of international and national competitions to find the best in the profession. Responsible for the cellar* and the wine service in top-class restaurants, the sommelier has the demanding task of matching the flavor of great wines with the sophisticated recipes of ambitious chefs. Finding a wine that can accompany or even enhance the myriad dishes ordered for a single table can pose something of a challenge. Without going through an affected ritual, a good sommelier should be able to advise diners with wit and elegance, and above all should seek to whet their curiosity. Sommeliers also have to monitor the quality of the wine chosen, eliminate "corked" bottles* (where the taste of the cork has contaminated the wine), be aware when a wine needs decanting*, carefully supervise the temperature of the wine, and choose the moment when it should be served. Though a new generation of sommeliers has breathed fresh life into the profession with their enthusiasm and passion for wine, all too many restaurants, even some of the most prestigious, show carelessness and negligence in their service of wine. However, the relative affluence of many households leading to an increase in "eating out" has led many restaurants to change their style. ER

The cellar at the Ritz Hotel, Paris, in 1968. Photograph Bruno Barbey.

Facing page: Terrain in th Tavel viney Rhône va' France.

Vineyard,
Thelema
Mountain at
Stellenbosch,
South Africa.

■ South Africa

South Africa, the seventh largest producer* in the world, is at one and the same time one of the oldest and one of the most recent countries on the wine map. It is no newcomer, since its position on the route to the Indies meant that colonists planted vines there in the mid-seventeenth century, and several wines, such as Constantia, have been famous for nearly 150 years. Yet the trade is still in its infancy since its political isolation up until 1989 excluded it from the revolution in winegrowing and wine-making that took place in the 1980s (replanting with healthy rootstock, maturing in cask, airconditioning, and so on).

Even today, less than a fifth of the production undergoes vinification* on the estate—the cooperatives run by the government's national KWV consortium control the rest. Most of the vineyards are to be found at the Cape, the dominant grape varieties being white* Chenin blanc and Palomino, and red* Cinsault, and the Cinsault x Pinot noir cross (pinotage). More recently, varieties such as Chardonnay and Cabernet sauvignon have been planted and the efforts made by the best estates have seen exports consistently on the rise. DLCDF

■ South America

Straddling the Andes, Chile and Argentina are the dominant players of South American viticulture, though each for rather different reasons. With its 1,600 million liters, Argentina is far

the grape. The wine revolution Chile has undergone over the last ten years is due to an open-mindedness to influences from abroad, especially from France, both in terms of investment and the oenologists* that now oversee the whole vinification* process (the famous "flying winemakers"). Selection of grape varieties has been entirely rethought: the Pais, the rather nondescript local grape, is being replaced by Cabernet sauvignon, while both the Merlot and the Chardonnay seem to hold great promise. The modernization of wine-making equipment, the increasing attention paid to the type of soil under vine, and the control over the yield are three note-worthy factors in this renais-sance. Valleys such as Maipo (near Santiago) for reds*, or Casablanca for whites*, are today drunk far afield. DLCDF

Vineyard on the Errazuriz estate, Chile.

and away the greatest producer* on the continent, and is ranked fifth worldwide. Almost all the wine it made used to be con-sumed at home, but nowadays it is an up-and-coming exporter and has a good reputation in the rest of the world.

Chile, with only a quarter of the area Argentina has under vines, has seen its exports rise almost tenfold in around a decade, and today they account for approximately half the total yield. Chile enjoys a wonder-fully contrasted climate*: very low rainfall that serves to dis-courage parasites, effective irri-gation that furthers growth, warm days that aid maturing, and cool air from the Andes to keep it in check. These factors combine to guarantee rich har-vests of good quality that preserve all the freshness of

■ SOUTHWEST FRANCE

The renown of Bordeaux* overshadows the quality of other wines in southwest France. Every time their wineries—in the triangle formed by the towns of Bergerac, Pau and Albi and some way distant from the sea—try to make a name for themselves, they come up against the eagle-eyed authority of their powerful neighbor. Yet the names found in their list of grape varieties are a powerful echo of the *terroir*: Tannat, Duras, Courbu, Malbec, Mauzac, Len-de-l'el, Manseng, Négrette, Arrufiac, Braucol, Fer servadou. The Southwest is proud of its historic varietals and of the perfect way its straightforward wines match the characteristic local cuisine*, their rustic authenticity traditionally enhancing the natural produce of the region. To the north, the terraces of the Dordogne planted with Bordeaux regional varieties provide wines such as Montravel (white*), Bergerac (red*, rosé*, and white), Pécharmant (red), and Monbazillac (liqueur wines*) that rival the Bordeaux wines.

Along the banks of the Garonne, the vineyards of Marmande, Buzet, and Fronton, hampered for a long time by the way Bordeaux controlled river traffic, proclaim their specialty, but they have found it hard to become well known outside the region in spite of very reasonable pricing. Only the historic Gaillac vineyard has acquired a measure of fame for its mauzac white wines* (dry, often slightly sparkling or sweetish).

The region's reputation today rests on its more remote districts, such as Cahors, whose spicy concentration and robust structure comes from the Malbec grape variety. A wine that ages well, but can equally be drunk young and lightly chilled with a beefsteak or *cassoulet* (a bean stew with duck), however, it is a joy not to be missed. Even better, perhaps, are wines from Béarn: Jurançon provides splendid, soft yet fresh whites, made from Petit manseng for the finest, and blended with Courbu and Manseng for the less sophisticated and drier wines. As for the red Madiran, the grape variety from which it was originally grown—the potent Tannat—has been toned down to produce one of the greatest of all French wines. DLCDF and PÉD

"When poor, reach for happiness,
Drink the secret wine.
This is the secret goal of philosophers,
And makes us rich."

Hafiz, Persian poet, c. 1320–1389

Cahors vineyard, near Luzech,
in the valley of the Lot.

■ Spain

Known as the "country of the grapevine," with 20 percent of Europe's total surface of vineyards, it only produces half the wine that France does. Yields are lower since the vines are often quite old and the climate* tough, with biting winters following dry, torrid summers. Apart from the south, which has long had a reputation for Jerez, i.e. sherry (a "fortified wine"), two regions stand out: Rioja and the valley of the Duero, though they do not have the same dynamism.

The presence of the French in Rioja from the time of the phylloxera crisis surely contributed considerably to the production of wines of quality. Grapes which for the most part come from all over the region (Rioja Alta for the subtlest and Rioja Alevesa for the richest), and various varieties* (Garnacha, Graciano, Tempranillo, etc.) are bought from the winegrowers by wine shippers who blend them to ensure the most consistent quality possible. Lengthy maturing in cask (up to ten years for Gran Reserva) is perhaps in keeping with Spanish taste, but is more and more avoided for export wines. Two appellations from the Duero valley have recently acquired a certain reputation: Rueda whites* retain their finesse due to a specially adapted *terroir*; Ribera del Duero reds*, which use the traditional *tinto del pais* as well as grape varieties from the Bordeaux region, mature slowly thanks to the cool nights (it is there that the celebrated domaine* of Vega Sicilia is located). DLCDF

Vineyard at the Vega Sicilia estate on the Duero, Spain.

■ SPARKLING WINES: "Beaded bubbles winking at the brim..." (John Keats)

Sparkling wines are for the most part obtained by putting a base wine in a thick glass bottle* and adding sugar and yeast so as to encourage secondary fermentation*. The carbon dioxide cannot escape, and dissolves in the wine; it will form an effervescent "froth" when the bottle is opened. If there is a rise above three degrees of atmospheric pressure, the French term for the wine is *mousseux*, while below that level the wine is known as *pétillant* ("lightly sparkling"), which in France has a limited appeal.

The enduring model of the champagne method follows strict rules from harvest* to maturing in the *cave* (cellar). Vinification occurs in two stages: the making of the generally light and acidic base wine, and the secondary fermentation with an added dose of sugar that gives around six degrees of atmospheric pressure. The bottles are then placed in special racks (*pupitres*) and gently shaken and turned each day to channel the sediment into the neck of the bottle. They are then "disgorged" (to expel the sediment adhering to the cork) and topped up with *liqueur d'expédition* (a "shipping liqueur," made of aged wine or brandy) with more or less sugar content depending on the type of champagne desired: *extra-brut* (bone dry), *brut* (dry), *sec* (slightly sweet), or *demi-sec* (sweet).

All this can equally take place in bulk containers, as is the case for sparkling wines produced in sealed vats, but the quality is inferior. A simpler, ancestral method is to bottle the base wine before its own natural fermentation has finished, and then the fermentation continues in the bottle: Gaillac, Clairette de Die, and Blanquette de Limoux are produced in this way. DLCDF

Champagne bottle held upside down before disgorging.

97

■ TASTING
Sensual Delights

Failing to give wine sufficient time and attention before swallowing it is to deprive oneself of one of its essential pleasures. There are schools and even university courses that teach the art of wine-tasting. The cardinal rules are captured in a passage by the French author Colette. "It is a time for quiet, for raising a plump-bellied, narrow-mouthed glass to the vaulted roof; first the eye, then the nose, finally the mouth…." Silence aids concentration, though daylight is better than a wine-cellar*, and the glass too should be carefully chosen.

Let the senses take their turn. First, one examines the *robe* (color): the intensity and nuances of color, clarity, and brilliance. Then the wine should be breathed in. The nose alerts us to anomalies and opens up a vast, hidden world of the senses. There are three stages: an initial sniff; a second breathing in after having swirled the wine in the glass to allow the scent to develop; the third should come after a pause, when the "nose" of the wine has developed. Three scents can be distinguished: the primary (from the grape variety*), the secondary (from the way it was made), and the tertiary (the "bouquet," which comes from the way the wine has developed). These scents make up the olfactory "families": flowers, fruits, spices, animal scents (game, musk); or vegetable odors (hay, humus, truffle); balsamic (resin, pine); or empryeumatic (smoky, grilled, tar, coffee), not forgetting the "bad" smells (sulfur, acetone, etc.).

In the mouth, our tastebuds will be alerted to the wine's "attack," its balance (between acidity, tannins, and alcohol), its "length" (of aftertaste), and a whole range of tactile and taste sensations. These communicate with the nasal cavities (retro-olfaction) and can be reinforced by breathing in a little air through the mouth. The taster can then spit out the wine—and the amateur swallow it. Only then is the drinker truly entitled to talk about the wine. TT

Terroir

Though the word can become a cliché if bandied about—above all when it serves as a disguise for mediocre or even downright bad wines—the notion of the *terroir* is the basis of the entire French appellation system. It covers the whole range of influences of a specific site on the life of the vine. These factors give the wine its distinct character, and make a Volnay different from a Vosne-Romanée, a Montrachet distinct from a Corton-Charlemagne.

Essentially, the influences are the soil*, the microclimate (see Climate), and the topography, which together determine the hydrological characteristics of the site, and the amount of sunshine annually. The differences between two *terroirs* can also stem from the varieties* planted, the winegrower's techniques and vine management*, and finally the type of vinification chosen, which can either bring out these inherent peculiarities, or, on the contrary, mask them entirely.

In Europe, classification* systems try to identify those *terroirs* blessed by nature with that additional touch of individuality that distinguishes the finest wines. However, the idea of *terroir* is little recognized in the New World wine producers—Australia, South America, and the United States and so on—which tend to harbor the suspicion that Europe has concocted the whole concept of the *terroir* simply in order to protect its markets from outside competition. ER and DLCDF

Facing page:
Philippe Mercier (1689–1760), *Young Man Tasting Wine.* Oil on canvas. Musée du Louvre, Paris.

Clos Saint-Jacques, Gevrey-Chambertin, France.

Napa Valley
vineyard
(California).

■ The United States

The United States occupies a place apart in the wine-growing world. The fourth largest wine producer, not far behind the big three (Italy*, France, and Spain*), it differs greatly from them in exporting a negligible amount, in terms of volume if not value. The high price* of American wine means that it is drunk almost exclusively within the country. The lion's share is made in the state of California, which has played the leading role in the sector since the time of the pioneers.

Traditional grape varieties, with the exception of Zinfandel, produce rather ordinary wines. More recent plantings of European varieties such as Cabernet sauvignon, Merlot, Chardonnay, and Sauvignon blanc—thanks to the work of oenologists* and sizable sums in investment—have seen a spectacular improvement in the quality of the wines produced. Following the tenets of the famous Davis University near San Francisco, which contend that the only factor determining the quality of grapes is temperature, five climatic* zones have been established. The two with the most sunshine are unsuitable for fine wines and so are dedicated to table and liqueur wines* (see Fortified Wines). It is, naturally, in the three remaining zones that the famous regions of the Napa and Sonoma Valleys are to be found: the cooling air from the Pacific Ocean makes the growing of great wines possible, and some are comparable to the very best in Europe. DLCDF

VARIETIES
Vitis Euvitis vinifera

Historically speaking, all grape varieties derive from spontaneous cross-fertilization or genetic mutations of members of the subgenus *Euvitis* of the genus *Vitis*, a huge group of climbing plants. Owing to continental drift, the *Euvitis* subgenus has split into two populations: the American, whose *rupestris* or *riparia* species have been used as rootstock (all French vines were grafted after the phylloxera disaster), and the Eurasian. The latter contains the species *vinifera* from which almost all wine-grape varieties descend.

The science of ampelography (the study of grape varieties) has identified several thousand varieties, but only a few hundred are used to make wine (they are in general not the same as table or raisin grapes). Among these, around thirty play a significant role, either in terms of quality or of quantity: Cabernet sauvignon, Chardonnay, Syrah, etc.

Due to the large number of diseases* that began to appear in the late nineteenth century, purely "vegetative" plant breeding has been gradually replaced by cloning. This laboratory-based method consists of the selection of the most worthwhile representative of a particular variety according to a number of criteria: absence of viruses, resistance to climatic conditions* and to gray rot, high yield, etc. The chosen one is then cloned to produce an entirely homogenous breed. The risk lies in the eventual degradation of the genetic pool of each variety and in the possible emergence of yet another disease that would be able to lay waste entire vineyards at a stroke. DLCDF

Bartolommeo
Bimbi
(1648–1725),
*Twenty-eight
Grape Varieties.*
Oil on canvas.
Galleria Palatina,
Palazzo Pitti,
Florence.

Bunch of Sauvignon grapes.

◼ Vinegar

The ordinary tipple of the Roman legions was wine vinegar generously mixed with water, and it was this that the centurion offered Christ on the Cross. It continued to be drunk by medieval peasants for centuries afterward, a certain taste for sourness being universal among all classes of society at the time, as many recipes from the Middle Ages* demonstrate.

To make vinegar it is enough to leave wine exposed to air in a broached wine barrel, especially if the weather is on the warm side.

By the end of the sixteenth century, the vinegar- and mustard-makers of Orléans, for example, had already acquired a solid reputation. Tastes came to prefer wine to vinegar though, and Dutch wine shippers had discovered through a process of trial and error that wine kept better when brandy was added, and when the barrel was treated with sulfur and regularly topped up. In 1865, Louis Pasteur isolated the vinegar "germ" and managed to destroy it by heating—the process that is now known as pasteurization. Nowadays, perhaps because of the greater amount of filtering that takes place, it is not always enough to empty out the dregs of your wine bottles into a keg to make good vinegar. To speed up the process, it is better to get hold of some quality "mother of vinegar," to act as the "yeast." TT

◼ Vine Life Cycle

In certain areas of South America, vines fruit constantly but are rapidly exhausted. In the more temperate regions of France, however, the seasons are clear-cut and the grapevine follows an annual vegetative cycle whose exact calendar depends both on the soil* and on the specific microclimate of each vineyard.

In France, the cycle can be said to begin after pruning when water drops form on the cane-ends around February/March ("weeping"), constituting the first visible sign of renewed root activity as the earth warms up. Once the mean temperature exceeds around 50°F (10°C) for several days in March/April, the buds begin to break and soon the green tips push through.

The growing phase lasts around four months. The leaves are followed by puny "embryo" clusters that then flower in June; fruit-set follows the fertilization of the flowers. The bunches of grapes remain green and extremely sour until the fruit changes color, a sign of ripening that generally occurs in August. It should be borne in mind that, during this whole time, the growing branches and foliage compete with the fruit for the sugars created through the photosynthesis at work in the leaves. From August, and until the leaves fall, the still green branches tend slowly to turn woody (lignification) and stock up on starch. After the harvest*, the vine loses its leaves. Thanks to its starch reserves, the plant will withstand the rigors of winter during its dormant period and is able to put out shoots once more the following spring. DLCDF

■ VINIFICATION: Wine or Vinegar

The term "vinification" refers to the group of processes following the harvest, from when the grapes arrive at the winery until the time when they finish their fermentation*. The quality of the harvest (the grapes should be ripe and free of rot) is obviously the key factor in determining the quality of the future wine. The vinification operations differ depending on whether the method for red*, white,* or rosé* is adopted, whether the wine is to be liqueur*, or fortified*, and whether it is matured in vats or oak* casks. The natural tendency of grape juice is to become moldy and to turn more or less simultaneously into vinegar* or wine. Though observed for centuries, the process only began to be properly understood in the nineteenth century* thanks to the efforts of Louis Pasteur. The antiseptic and antioxidant properties of sulfur, a substance used for centuries in an experimental way, are today better controlled. Progress made by oenology* now allows winegrowers to transform grapes into a wine that can justifiably be described as "fine," completely different from the alcoholic, acidic beverages known to the ancient world* or to the Middle Ages*, which had to be sweetened with honey or mixed with salt water. Depending on the country or region concerned, vinification methods differ widely, and some may even be prohibited. The best known are chaptalization (the adding of sugar to the must which then ferments, with a proportionate increase in the degree of alcohol) in warm zones where grapes ripen poorly, and acidification in regions where they lack liveliness. DLCDF

■ Vins Doux Naturels

These "naturally sweet wines" (VDN) are fortified wines* produced—in certain *Appellation d'Origine Contrôlée* (AOC) districts in the South of France—from varieties such as Grenache, Muscat, Malvoisie (Malmsey), and Maccabeo. "Fortification" takes place during fermentation so as to preserve some of the natural grape sugars. The process increases the alcohol level of the wine which can reach 15 to 18 degrees (less than port, which can reach 20 degrees), and gives it a velvety texture and an aromatic richness, marrying honey, mint, and citrus notes in the case of the whites*,

and more complex fig, spice, and cocoa for the reds*. Two methods of wine-making leave their mark on the unique flavor of red VDNs. Vintage or *rimage* ("age of the grape" in Catalan) wine is sometimes aged in an airtight, enclosed space (like a dry wine) so it keeps a deep color and lively, spicy red fruit. Another, more common method is to encourage oxidation: the wine is matured in contact with the air in empty casks, and sometimes exposed to the sun in glass carboys. The resulting *rancio* style is characterized by a mahogany color and candied fruit flavor with delicious nut and roasted coffee overtones.

The majority of white VDNs are produced in the Languedoc-Roussillon region in southern France: these include the Muscats from the towns of Frontignan, Lunel, Mireval, Rivesaltes, Saint-Jean-de-Minervois, etc. But the Rhône valley* also boasts a particularly honeyed example, the Muscat de Beaumes-de-Venise. As for the reds, the Grenache noir cultivated on the shale soils of Maury and Banyuls in Roussillon give balanced wines of character that can hold their own against port. Less well known is the red VDN from the Rasteau AOC in the southern Rhône valley, which is also made from the Grenache variety. ER

Château de
Pommard, 1988.

■ Vintage Years

The art of cultivating vines is full of pitfalls. It depends on climatic conditions; it is at the mercy of spring frost, diseases and parasites, variable quantities of sunshine and rain, and harvesting too early—or too late. All these factors can make picking healthy, ripe grapes—the essential raw material for any great vintage—a thankless task. So it is that the *millésime* indicated on the label* (that is, the year of the grape harvest*) gives more information than one might at first think. From it can be deduced the weather conditions specific to each region that accompanied the year's vine life cycle* up to and including the grape harvest (September/October in the northern hemisphere, and February/April in the southern hemisphere). It is crucial to avoid the obvious trap of judging all vintages by the yardstick of the most famous Bordeaux*. Fine wines are nowadays nearly all labeled with a vintage year, except for the majority of champagnes*, which are often a blend* of several years. ER

■ Vocabulary

Wine loosens even the most reluctant tongues and has, over the centuries, given rise to a rich vocabulary, dominated by metaphor. As wine historian Martine Châtelain-Courtois remarked, wine "tells us a great deal about our civilization [ ], it is the center of and the pretext for a veritable encyclopedia in which religion, nature, and the cosmos, the body, life, and death, sexuality and aesthetics, society and politics all have a place." There are words for sensations and tastes, there is the language of drunkenness*, the vocabulary of the elite, and the expressions used by ordinary folk. There are the flowery phrases used in poetry about wine, and there are

technical analyses. Since 1970, however, wine specialists have been engaged in normalizing tasting* terms. The very complexity of the subject and, in spite of all efforts to the contrary, its ultimately subjective nature, mean that professional oenologists themselves are occasionally forced to fall back on images. Whether it be in the mouth of a thirteenth-century street-seller, who pronounced his wine "quaffable, full and with body, running like a squirrel through the wood, dry and lively, as bright as a sinner's tear," or in that of a modern-day wine lover delighting in a glass of Pomerol whose aroma is of "undergrowth and truffles," and which seems on the palate, "full, fat, rich, winey, and round-bodied, with melty tannins and a delicate chocolatey-oak flavor," one hears the same expressions of wonderment at this mysterious gift of Nature which, to our immense pleasure, is renewed year after year. TT

Albert Fourié,
Wedding at Yport,
1886.
Oil on canvas.
Musée des Beaux-Arts, Rouen.

Facing page:
De-stalking
prior to pressing.
Château Haut-
Brion,
Pessac-Léognan
vineyard, France.

■ WHITE WINES: IN PRAISE OF SPEED

White wines are for the most part made from white-skinned grapes (grape flesh is always "white") that are pressed immediately to prevent the quality being adversely affected by lengthy exposure to air, since oxidation turns the juice brownish. To make pressing easier, the grapes may be given a preliminary crushing: the split fruit release their juice more readily. As the grapes are loaded into the wine-press, the juice that flows naturally from under it (the "free-run wine") is collected into a vat which is then filled with the juice from one, or sometimes two, pressings.

Sulfur compounds are generally added during vatting: sulfur has an anti-oxidizing effect but is also an indispensable antiseptic that reduces the activity of the various fermenting yeasts*. The vats are left to stand for at least half a day to let the lees settle: this process, called *débourbage*, allows the coarser lees (the pieces of grape skin and pulp, and odd particles of soil) that might give the wine a bad taste, to fall to the bottom of the vat. Then, depending on the type of wine and the quality required, the clarified juice is transferred to a new vat or into oak casks* where it undergoes fermentation to turn it into alcohol. DLCDF

■ Wine Bars

A wine bar is, for the most part, a bistro, tapas bar, or little restaurant that serves unpretentious dishes and where business focuses on a wide but select range of wines also sold by the glass*. Some also act as wine merchants and sell bottles that can be first tasted at the counter.

All too often, however, the "wine bar" sign serves as a trap to the unwary, hanging as it does over a place where the wine is poorly chosen and badly treated. The best examples, however, are not snobbish eateries serving overpriced Bordeaux to rows of label-obsessed drinkers, but havens offering new horizons, and friendly, good-humored service. Nothing can replace the passion of the owner as he or she guides customers and whets their curiosity. Best of all is a wine bar filled with a lively, intelligent choice of wines served in a happy and unstuffy atmosphere. ER

■ Wine Fairs

In the last few years, the wine fair has become one of the main events in the wine lover's calendar when the industry starts up again after the long summer break. This period accounts for up to 30 percent of turnover in the French wine sector, for instance, and many store chains produce catalogs and eye-catching advertisements to attract connoisseurs and amateurs who are on the look-out for bargains. The opening day is invariably a feeding-frenzy that for the best lots can turn into a scrimmage, since, all too often, the good wines sold as "loss-leaders" appear only in minute quantities amongst stacks of mediocre wines. As always, the watchword is let the buyer beware.

Many wine fairs and auctions concentrate on Bordeaux* (between 50 and 100 percent of the wines on offer); the customer is well-advised to do the same and steer clear of poorly selected wines from other regions, such as Burgundy*. An important turning-point lies ahead, however. After the return of good and highly prized vintages* (1995 and 1996), and the boom in prices for new wines, numerous Bordeaux châteaux have turned to large-scale retail outlets to protect their margins as well as their prestige. Consequently, in the future there will be fewer prestigious *crus* and increasing numbers of (often perfectly drinkable) "second labels," but bargains based on famous labels will become harder to find. The serious wine lover should be prepared to adopt new buying strategies, experimenting with other regions, which could result in a better selection of wines at a more reasonable price. ER

Wine-making and Maturing

The new wine, straight after fermentation,* is far from having developed its qualities to the full, and still requires the stage known as *élevage.*

This can be defined as the art of encouraging the wine to blossom to its full potential before bottling. For the simplest wines, the process begins after malolactic fermentation with an initial racking to drain off the lees (miniscule suspended particles that fall slowly to the bottom) and ends when it has stayed in a vat until the following year. Muscadet is a special case since it is "matured" on its lees so as to preserve maximum freshness. During

wine-making, various clarifying techniques are used so the wine acquires the purity demanded by the consumer. The centrifugal press eliminates the yeast; cold stabilization makes the tartar fall as little crystals to the bottom of the cask or vat; fining with egg-white or fish-glue draws off the sediment; finally, racking (transferring the wine from one vat to another to aerate it) makes it more homogenous, eliminates the carbon dioxide, and separates off the deposits left by fining.

It is, of course, for wines aged in oak casks—always after fermentation for reds*, though sometimes before this for whites*—that the term of *élevage* acquires its full meaning. Each cask is looked after individually: it is regularly topped up (i.e. wine is added to compensate for increases in ullage, that is loss through evaporation or absorption into the wood) and stirred to disperse the sediment that nourishes the wine, and then the wine is racked again from cask to cask to keep it well aerated. Fine-tuning these apparently simple operations, and the frequency with which they are performed during any given vintage* demands immense skill. The greatness of a wine depends for a large part on the quality of the wine-making. DLCDF

Wine sale at the Beaune Hospice, eastern France. Photograph Henri Cartier-Bresson.

Racking a barrel in the Domecq cellars, Jerez, Spain.

■ Wine Shops, Taverns and Guinguettes

Wine has been drunk publicly all over Europe for centuries. The earliest of the *guinguettes* appeared around 1650. These partially open-air wine shops also sold food and, located just outside the walls of the city, were cheaper than their counterparts inside the walls as they were exempt from the prohibitive tolls of the Middle Ages*. Initially, it was mainly the lower orders who flocked to these less genteel districts to drink unsophisticated wines. Louis-Sébastien Mercier, in his vast fresco of city life, *Le Tableau de Paris* (1781–89) characterized these as "bitter, coarse, and hateful." Later, craftsmen, girls of doubtful virtue, and even the lower-middle classes also made their joyous way to these low-rent establishments that had

equivalents in other cities elsewhere. Gaming, dancing, and drinking rubbed shoulders with prostitution, fist fights, and wine-trafficking. Churchmen often condemned such promiscuity, but the population naturally paid little heed to them. The *Guinguettes* later became associated with the Impressionists (Renoir's painting of the *Moulin de la Galette*, for example) and much decadent—or nostalgic—literature and film.

Elsewhere, William Harrison's *Description of England* (1587) relates that "in all our inns we have plenty of ale, beer and sundry kinds of wine." The great age of the wine shop was during the following century, though another traveler, Donald Lupton, has a traditional ale-house keeper call the new style of wine-tavern "an upstart outlandish fellow,"

Vincent van Gogh. *Guinguette at Montmartre*, 1886. Oil on canvas. Musée d'Orsay, Paris.

fifty years later. The Restoration ushered in a great age of public drinking with peers such as the poet Lord Rochester frequenting high and low establishments alike. By the mid-to-late eighteenth century, however, the battle was between (low) gin and (decent) beer, as satirized in Hogarth's paintings, and wine took a back seat as a publicly consumed drink (except in gentlemen's clubs). In the last thirty years, wine has made a comeback with the vogue for eating in restaurants and wine-bars*. TT

■ Wine Tours and Tourism

Drinking a glass of wine, one often feels the desire to travel to the vineyard and learn more about the history, geography, and architecture of the region, and even to meet with some of the winegrowers. In northern Europe, wine is so closely associated in the public imagination with vacations and sun that it is no surprise that tourists heading for the sun-kissed countryside should make a detour to a local vineyard or two. Although wine tourism has gone from strength to strength in the last couple of decades, it is by no means a new phenomenon. At the end of the eighteenth century*, the enthusiastic wine lover, Thomas Jefferson, traveled the length and breadth of Europe studying vineyards and tasting their produce. Certain wine-growing regions, such as the Loire* in France and the Rhine or Mosel in Germany* have long benefited from the existing tourist infrastructure to promote their wares. Surprisingly, the Bordeaux* region began to use tourism as a promotional and

public relations tool rather late in the day. Nonetheless, an estate such as Château Pichon-Longueville today receives more than 100,000 visitors a year.

The elite Bordeaux châteaux, however, tend to discourage or even flatly refuse impromptu visits, preferring groups with a specialist guide. Elsewhere, the individual approach can pay dividends, especially if one has the courtesy to telephone beforehand. Such a visit takes place in a more relaxed atmosphere and allows for direct contact with the winegrower and the opportunity to buy some wine on the spot. One should beware, however, of impulse buying in the heat of the moment. And watch your step in those dark cellars—especially on the way out! ER

Historic wine-presses in the cloisters at Eberbach, Eltville in the Rheingau, Germany.

V A R I E T I E S

The Principal Grape Varieties

Red varieties

Cabernet sauvignon: Planted all over the world, it is first and foremost one of Bordeaux's* most famous varieties, especially for Médoc growths. It gives a deep, rich color, good tannin, and a full aroma. Its primary aromas of red berries evolve into more complex notes as it ages (cedar, violet, etc.).

Cabernet franc: A cousin of Cabernet sauvignon, it gives slightly less delicate, but still richly aromatic, wines. The second variety in Saint-Émilion and Pomerol, it is also cultivated in the Loire* and in South America*.

Carignan: This variety occupies one-fifth of France's wine-growing area and is most prevalent in less costly wines from the south of the country. It gives well-colored and tannic wines, but without great character, unless the grapes come from old vines.

Gamay: This is the Beaujolais'* favorite variety, with a reputation for fruity, supple young wines with not much tannin. It should be noted that California's Gamay-beaujolais is in fact an insipid clone of Pinot noir.

Grenache noir: This variety gives high-alcohol wines, such as Châteauneuf-du-Pape in the Rhône valley, Coteaux-du-Languedoc or else fortified wines, like the famous Banyuls. As it is particularly strong, it is often blended with other varieties.

Malbec: Its color and high tannin enhances many Bordeaux blends*, and is characteristic of Cahors (where it is known as Auxerrois). It is today one of the most important varieties cultivated in Argentina, much appreciated for an alcohol content which withstands the pressure of high yields.

Merlot: This is the dominant grape in the areas that produce Saint-Émilion and Pomerol, and gives them a soft, velvety character. It forms 95 percent of Château Pétrus, the greatest Pomerol growth and one of the world's most expensive wines.

Mourvèdre: A late-maturing variety which needs a deal of warmth, it gives well-structured wines, with a good color, and blackcurrant, blackberry, leather, and meat aromas. The main variety used for Bandol, it is also grown in Provence*, in the southern Rhône* valley, and increasingly, in Languedoc-Roussillon*.

Nebbiolo: The great Piedmont wines, Barolo and Barbaresco, are made solely from this Italian variety. It is characterized by a strong structure with considerable finesse and can make for fine laying-down wines.

Pinot noir: This is the main variety in Burgundy, an area in which it flourishes. At its best, it gives sensual wines with a rich bouquet, and a fine, velvet texture.

Sangiovese: With its cherry and plum aroma, this is the main variety in Tuscan Chianti.

Syrah: The dominant grape in the red growths of the northern Rhône * valley, it gives full-bodied, strong wines with fruit aromas (strawberry, blackcurrant), and a scent of violets, sometimes spicy.

Tannat: This original variety produces the strong and tannin-rich Madiran wines from Southwest France.

Tempranillo: This is the variety that makes Rioja and Ribera del Duero in Spain*.

Zinfandel: A variety of unknown origin grown mostly in California (it is also to be found in Australia*).

Good vintage years from 1945-1999 ranked (out of 20).

By Jean-Claude and Valérie Vrinat, assisted by Nicolas Bonnot, Sommelier at Taillevent.

	1945	1947	1953	1955	1959	1961	1966	1969	1970	1971	1975	1976	1978
Red Bordeaux	19	18	18	17	16	19	17	11	18	16	16	15	17
White Bordeaux	19	17	16	17	16	18	15	13	17	15	17	18	15
Red Burgundy	18	17	14	15	16	18	16	18	10	17	8	16	18
White Burgundy	14	16	15	16	16	16	16	17	13	16	11	15	18
Champagne	18	18	17	17	17	18	17	16	15	16	17	16	16
Alsace	18	17	17	16	18	17	15	15	15	18	13	18	15
Côtes du Rhône	17	16	13	15	14	17	16	13	17	15	13	17	19
Loire	17	19	16	15	17	16	14	16	14	16	14	18	16
Jura	16	18	15	15	16	16	14	16	12	15	14	17	14
Languedoc/Provence													

It makes full-bodied, spicy reds, with aromas of strawberry, raspberry, wild blackberry. It also produces rather insipid whites and rosés.

White Varieties

Airén: This is the most widely cultivated variety in the world. Its principal advantage is an ability to resist the drought conditions on the vast plains of Spain's* La Mancha.

Chardonnay: The most famous white variety of all. In Champagne*, it is used in blends based on Pinot noir or Pinot meunier and produces Blanc de Blanc, with a taste of white berries, hazelnuts, and sometimes lemon. In Burgundy*, it is usually the only grape variety used to produce the great white wines that reach incomparable complexity in the vineyards of Chablis, Puligny-Montrachet and Corton-Charlemagne.

Chenin blanc: The white variety in the Loire*, its characteristic acidity can give wines that can be kept for a long time. It also produces sweeter *moelleux* whites, if the grapes are harvested when at the peak of ripeness. Supreme examples of these are Savennières and Coteaux-de-Layon.

Gewürztraminer: The variety for the Alsace wine of the same name, that is plump, opulent, and highly individual (bouquets include rose and lychees, with spicy overtones).

Marsanne: In conjunction with Roussane, it gives some great white wines in the north of the Rhône valley, Hermitage in particular. The wines are full-bodied when marsanne predominates, but more delicate when Roussane has the edge. Characteristic aromas are acacia honey and hazelnut.

Muscat: This grapevine has numerous varieties, some of which produce fine table grapes. Muscat wines feature a strong "grapey" flavor. Muscat d'Alsace, a white with floral notes, and Muscat de Beaumes-de-Venise (southern Rhône valley), a highly aromatic sweet white, are both blends of white and rosé *muscats à petits grains*.

Pinot gris: The Alsace first growth Tokay-Pinot gris owes its reputation and its astonishing fullness to this grape variety. Its primary aromas of peach and apricot give way to honey notes when it is matures.

Riesling: The classic white grape in Alsace and Germany, its most favored region is Mosel-Saar-Ruwer, where it produces elegant, fruity wines with mineral notes (gasoline, naphthalene), that have

considerable fullness. Riesling TBA is one of the truly great liqueur wines.

Sauvignon blanc: This is the most popular white variety in the central Loire, where its two most illustrious wines are Pouilly-Fumé and Sancerre, with their marked redcurrant aroma. It is also highly prized in New Zealand where the wines it produces are more exuberant in their bouquet, with exotic fruit notes (passionfruit, mango).

Sémillon: This grape is favored by the *Botrytis* fungus that produces noble rot. It produces softly sweet, almost unctuous wines, with honey and vanilla aromas, such as Sauternes in the Bordeaux region (in general blended with sauvignon). In Australia, on the other hand, it makes dry whites which age well.

Sylvaner: Cultivated principally in Alsace and Germany, it makes for simple, light wines that are pleasantly lively.

Viognier: From this variety come the famous dry whites of Condrieu, and Château-Grillet from the northern Rhône valley. They develop a richly floral bouquet, with characteristic flavors of apricot and peach.

☐ *Ready to drink.*   ☐ *May be too old.*   ☐ *For laying down.*

1982	1983	1985	1988	1989	1990	1991	1991	1992	1993	1994	1996	1998	1999	
18	16	17	17	18	18	14	14	13	15	16	17	16	15	Red Bordeaux
15	18	16	18	19	19	13	13	13	14	15	16	15	16	White Bordeaux
13	17	18	16	17	18	16	16	16	18	16	18	16	15	Red Burgundy
17	18	17	17	17	17	15	15	18	17	17	18	15	14	White Burgundy
17	16	17	17	16	18	14	14	15	14	14	17	13	16	Champagne
14	19	17	10	17	18	14	14	15	15	13	15	15	13	Alsace
14	18	18	17	17	18	15	15	16	14	15	17	18	16	Côtes du Rhône
14	17	17	17	19	18	13	13	14	16	15	17	15	15	Loire
12	18	17		17	18	15	15	15	14	15	16	17	15	Jura
						16	16	14	15	14	17	18	16	Languedoc/Provence

FRENCH WINES

A list of addresses limited to two or three per wine region is of necessity fairly arbitrary. In every wine district one can certainly find more prestigious, cheaper, or more original wines, by chance on one's travels or by consulting a detailed guidebook. At the following addresses, however, you will find wines of reliable quality from the best areas of each region, not always from the most famous names but from vineyards dedicated to producing delicious wines at reasonable prices.

ALSACE

Domaine Lucien Albrecht
68500 Orschwihr
Tel: 03 89 76 95 18

Domaine Paul Blanck et Fils
68240 Kientzheim
Tel: 03 89 78 23 56

BORDEAUX

Château Faugères
33330 Saint-Émilion
Tel: 05 57 40 34 99

Château Lamothe-Guignard
33210 Sauternes
Tel: 05 56 76 60 28

Château Tour-Haut-Caussan
33340 Blaignan
Tel: 05 56 09 00 77

BURGUNDY

Côte Chalonnaise
Antonin Rodet
71640 Mercurey
Tel: 03 85 98 12 12

Côte de Beaune
Domaine Tollot-Beaut
21200 Chorey-les-Beaune
Tel: 03 80 22 16 54

Côte de Nuits
Maison J. H. Faiveley
8, rue du Tribourg, B. P. 9
21701 Nuits-Saint-Georges
Tel: 03 80 61 04 55

Domaine Aubert et Pamela de Villaine
71150 Bouzeron
Tel: 03 85 91 20 50

Mâconnais
Domaine des Deux Roches
71960 Davaye
Tel: 03 85 35 86 51

BEAUJOLAIS

Domaine Pierre-Marie Chermette
69620 Saint-Vérand
Tel: 04 74 71 79 42

CHAMPAGNE

Pierre Gimonnet et Fils
51530 Cuis
Tel: 03 26 59 78 70

Champagne Jean Valentin
51500 Sacy
Tel: 03 26 49 21 91

JURA

Domaine Jean Macle
39210 Château-Chalon
Tel: 03 84 85 21 85

Domaine André et Mireille Tissot
39600 Montigny-les-Arsures
Tel: 03 84 66 08 27

LANGUEDOC-ROUSSILLON

Domaine d'Aupilhac
34150 Montpeyroux
Tel: 04 67 96 61 19

Domaine Cazes Frères
66600 Rivesaltes
Tel: 04 68 64 08 26

LOIRE

Domaine des Baumard
49190 Rochefort-sur-Loire
Tel: 02 41 78 70 03

Château de la Ragotière
44330 La Regrippière
Tel: 02 40 33 60 56

Domaine Pierre Druet
37140 Benais
Tel: 02 47 97 37 34

PROVENCE

Château de Pibarnon
83740 La Cadière-d'Azur
Tel: 04 94 90 12 73

Domaine Les Bastides
13610 Le-Puy-Sainte-Réparade
Tel: 04 42 61 97 66

RHÔNE

Domaine du Colombier
26600 Mercurol
Tel: 04 75 07 44 07

Domaine de l'Oratoire Saint-Martin
84290 Cairanne
Tel: 04 90 30 82 07

Domaine de Villeneuve
84100 Orange
Tel: 04 90 34 57 55

SAVOIE

Domaine Louis Magnin
73800 Arbin
Tel: 04 79 84 12 12

SUD-OUEST

Château d'Aydie
64330 Aydie
Tel: 05 59 04 08 00

Domaine Cauhapé
64360 Monein
Tel: 05 59 21 33 02

OTHER COUNTRIES

AUSTRALIA

Orlando Wines
AMain Road, Rowland Flat
SA 5352
Barossa Valley
Tel: 8-8521-3111
Fax: 8-85213-100
www.jacobscreek.com.au

Rosemount Estate
18 Herbert Street
2064 Artarmon, N.S.W.
Tel: 29-902-2100
Fax: 29-902-2199

Lindemans Wines of Australia
634 Princess Highway
Tempe, N.S.W.
Tel: 25-591-466
Fax: 25-593-488

CHILE

Vina Concha y Toro
Avenida Nueva Tajamar 481,
piso 15, Torre Sur
Vitacura, Santiago
Tel: 821-7300
Fax: 853-0024
esanfuentes@conchaytoro.cl

Vina Santa Rita
Hendaya 60
Office 202, Santiago
Tel: 362-2000
Fax: 228-6335
info@santarita.com

Vina Los Vascos
Benjamin No 2944
Office 31-Las Condes
3156 Santiago
Tel: 232-6633
Fax: 231-4373

GERMANY

Weingut Dr. Burklin-Wolf
Postfach 1165
D-67157 Wachenheim
Tel: 6322-95330
Fax: 6322-953-330

Weingut Johann Josef Prum
Uferallee 19
Bernkastel
D-54470 Wehlen/Mosel
Tel: 6531-3091
Fax: 6531-6071

ITALY

Castello di Volpaia
Loc. Volpaia
53017 Radda in Chianti (SI)
Tel: 577-738-066
Fax: 577-738-619
volpaia@chiantinet.it

Gaja
Via Torino 36
12050 Barbaresco (CN)
Tel: 1873-635-158
Fax: 173-635-256

Sassicaia
Bolgheri
57020 Livorno
Tel: 565-762-084
Fax: 565-762-017

PORTUGAL

Fonseca Guimaraens Vinhos
Rua Barao Forrester, 404
4401 Vila Nova de Gaia
Tel: 2-371-9999
Fax: 2-3707-321

W. & J. Graham & Co.
Apartado 19
4401 Vila Nova de Gaia
Tel: 2-379-6063
Fax: 2-301-922

SPAIN

Bodegas Martinez Bujanda
Camino Viejo s/n
01320 Oyon Alava
Tel: 94-112-2188
Fax: 4-122-111

Bodegas Torres
Comercio 22
08720 Vilafranca del Penedes
Barcelona
Tel: 93-817-7400
Fax: 93-817-7444
webmaster@torres.es

UNITED STATES

Columbia Crest
P. O. Box 1976
Woodinville, Washington
98072
Tel: 425-488-1133
Fax: 425-488-4657

Durney Organic Vineyards
69 West Carmel Valley Rd
Carmel Valley, CA 93924
Tel: 831-659-6220

Handley Cellars
3151 Hwy. 128
Philo, CA 95466
Tel: 800-733-3151

Hargrave Vineyard
North Country Road
Box 927
Cutchogue, NY 11935
Tel: 516-734-5111
Fax: 516-734-5485

Ponzi Vineyards
14665 SW Winery Lane
Beaverton
Oregon 97007
Tel: 503-628-1227
Fax: 503-628-0354

SPECIALIST WINESHOPS IN THE U.K.

Balls Brothers
313 Cambridge Heath Rd
London E2 9LQ
Tel: 0207 739 6466
www.ballsbrothers.co.uk

Adam Bancroft
East Bridge Office North
New Covent Garden Market
London SW5 5JB
Tel: 0207 627 8700

Cockburns of Leith
The Wine Emporium
7 Devon Place
Haymarket
Edinburgh EH12 5HJ
Tel: 0131 346 1113
www.winelist.co.uk

Corney & Barrow
12 Helmet Row
London EC1V 3QJ
Tel: 0207 251 4051
www.corbar1.demon.co.uk

Farr Vintners
19 Sussex St
London SW1V 4RR
Tel: 0207 821 2000
sales@farr-vintners.com

Fortnum & Mason
181 Picadilly
London W1A 1ER
Tel: 0207 734 8040
www.fortnumandmason.co.uk

Friarwood
26 New King's Rd
London SW6 4ST
Tel: 0207 736 2628
www.friarwood.com

Goedhuis & Co
6 Rudolf Place, Miles St
London SW8 1RP
Tel: 0207 793 7900
goedhuis@btinternet.com

Handford Wine
12 Portland Road
Holland Park
London W11 4LE
Tel: 0207 221 9614
www.handford-wine.demon.co.uk

Hedley Wright
11 Twyford Center
Bishop's Stortford
Herts CM23 3YT
Tel: 01279 506 512
Wine@hedleywright.com

Justerini & Brooks Ltd.
21 St. James Square
London SW1Y 4SS
Tel: 0207 484 6400

La Reserve
56 Walton Street

London SW3 1RB
Tel: 0207 978 5601

La Vigneronne
105 Old Brompton Rd
London SW7 EC2
Tel: 0207 589 6113

Lea & Sandeman
211 Kensington Church St
London W8 7LX
Tel: 0207 221 1982

Liberty Wines
Unit A53, New Covent
Garden Food Market
London SW8 5EE
Tel: 0207 720 5350
Fax: 0207 720 6158
order@libertywine.co.uk

Moreno Wines
11 Marylands Road
London W9 2DU
Tel: 0207 286 0678

Morris & Verdin
10 The Leathermarket
Weston St
London SE1 3ER
Tel: 0207 357 8866
info@m-v.co.uk

Raeburn Fine Wines
21/23 Comely Bank Road
Edinburgh, EH4 1DS
Tel: 0131 332 1159
raeburn@netcomuk.co.uk
www.raeburnfinewines.com

Roberson
348 Kensington High St
London W14 8NS
Tel: 0207 371 2121
wines@roberson.co.uk
www.roberson.co.uk

The English Wine Centre
Alfriston
East Sussex BN26 5QS
Tel: 01323 870 164
bottles@englishwine.co.uk
www.englishwine.co.uk

The RSJ Wine Company
115 Wootton St
London SE1 8LY
Tel: 0207 633 0881

Waterloo Wine Co
6 Vine Yard
London SE1 1QL
Tel: 0207 403 7967

SPECIALIST WINESHOPS IN THE U.S. (NEW YORK)

34th Street Winery
460 W. 34th St.
New York, NY 10001
Tel: 212 564 6830

Astor Wines & Spirits
12 Astor Place

New York, NY 10003
Tel: 212 674 7500

Chelsea Wine Vault
75 9th Ave
New York, NY 10011
Tel: 212 462 42-44

First Avenue Wines
383 1st Avenue
New York, NY 10010
Tel: 212 673 3600

Manley's Wine & Spirits
35 8th Avenue
New York, NY 10014
Tel: 212 242 3712

Morrell & Company
665 11th Ave
2nd Floor
New York, NY 10019
Tel: 212 688 9370

Nancy Wines
313 Columbus Ave
New York, NY 10023
Tel: 212 877 4040

New York Wine Exchange
9 Beaver St.
New York, NY 10004
Tel: 212 422 2222

Ninth Ave Vintner
669 9th Ave
New York, NY 10036
Tel: 212 664 9463

Park Avenue Liquors
292 Madison Ave
New York, NY 10017
Tel: 212 685 2442

Sutton Wine Shop
403 E. 57th St
New York, NY 10022
Tel: 212 755 6626

The Wine Gallery
576 6th Ave
New York, NY 10011
Tel: 212 242 2719

The Wine Shop
1585 1st Ave
New York, NY 10028
Tel: 212 517 2550

Union Square Wine
33 Union Sq W.
New York, NY 10003
Tel: 212 675 8100

Vino
143e 27th St.
New York, NY 10016
Tel: 212 725 6516

Windsor Wine Shop
1114 1st Avenue
New York, NY 10021
Tel: 212 308 1650

WINE MUSEUMS

FRANCE

Musée du Vin
rue d'Enfer
21200 Beaune
Tel: 03 80 22 08 19

Musée du Vin et de la Tonnellerie
12, rue Voltaire
37500 Chinon
Tel: 02 47 93 25 63

Musée de la Vigne et du Vin
3, rue Turgot
11200 Lezignan Corbières
Tel: 04 68 27 07 57

Musée des Arts et Métiers de la Vigne
Château Maucaillou
33480 Moulis en Médoc
Tel: 05 56 58 01 23

U.K.

Harvey's Wine Museum
12 Denmark Street,
Bristol BS1 5DQ
Tel: 0117 927 5036
Fax: 0117 927 5002

Vinopolis
1 Bank End
London SE1 9BU
www.vinopolis.co.uk

UNITED STATES

Cowie Wine Museum
101 N. Carbon City Road
Paris, Arkansas 72855
Tel: 1-800-419-2691-01
Email: cowie@cswnet.com

Napa Valley Wine Museum
55, President's Circle
Yountville, CA 94599
Tel:707-944-0500
www.napavalleymuseum.org

University of Pennsylvania Museum: History of Wine
33rd & Spruce Streets
Philadelphia, PA 19104
Tel: 215.898.4001
Fax: 215.898.0657

CANADA

The Wine Museum
1304 Ellis Street, Kelowna
B.C, V1Y 1Z8,
Tel: 250 868-0441
Fax: 250 763-5722

SEE ALSO
www.cyberbacchus.com
www.wines.com
www.grape-varieties.com
www.history-of-wine.com
www.winefiles.org

I N D E X

SELECTED BIBLIOGRAPHY

Broadbent, Michael. *Wine Vintages*. London: Antique Collectors Club, 1997.

Cobbold, David. *The Great Wines and Vintages*. New York: Chartwell Press, 1997.

Collombet, François. *The Flammarion Guide to World Wines*. Paris: Flammarion, 2000.

Desseauve, Thierry. *The Book of Wine*. Paris: Flammarion, 2001.

Foulkes, Christopher (ed.). *Larousse Encyclopedia of Wine*. Paris: Larousse, 1994.

Gabler, James. *Passions: the Wines and Travels of Thomas Jefferson*. Baltimore: Bacchus, 1995.

Johnson, Hugh. *The Story of Wine*. London: Mitchell Beazley, 1998.

Johnson, Hugh. *World Atlas of Wine*. New York: Simon & Schuster, 1994.

Lukacs, Paul. *American Vintage: The Rise of American Wine*. New York: Houghton Mifflin, 2000.

Robinson, Jancis. *The Oxford Companion to Wine*. New York: Oxford University Press, 1999.

Shaw Nelson, Kay. *All Along the Rhine*. New York: Hippocrene Books, 2001.

Stevenson, Tom. *Sotheby's World Wine Encyclopedia*. London: Dorling Kindersley, 1991.

Photographic credits: ANTWERP, Royal Museum of Fine Arts 101; FLORENCE, Galleria Palatina 43; FRANKFURT, Städelsches Kunstinstitut 94; LONDON, British Museum 86; MADRID, Museo del Prado 28; PARIS, Bibliothèque nationale de France 73, 84; Jacques Boulay cover, 20, 29 bottom; Dagli Orti 4–5, 27, 40, 71, 87 top, 100; Flammarion archives 58–9, 95; Hoa Qui/Jacques Bravo 102; P. Hussenot 111; Magnum/Elliott Erwitt 32–3 /Henri Cartier-Bresson 46, 69 /Erich Lessing 57 /Gilles Peress 90–1 /Bruno Barbey 103 bottom /Martine Franck 108–9; Réunion des musées nationaux 56, 67, 70, 79, 88–9; Ryman/Cabannes 6, 37; Scope 50, 87 bottom /Jean-Luc Barde 7, 8, 12, 13, 21, 30, 31, 36–7, 38–9, 63, 65, 85, 102, 105 /Jacques Guillard 9, 14, 19, 24–5, 28, 42, 45, 47, 54, 62, 64, 68, 74 bottom, 74–5 top, 83, 96–7, 107 /Michel Guillard 10, 16–7, 35, 41 bottom, 51, 64, 66 bottom, 78 /Gerd Kramer 22–3 top /Kactus 26 /Michel Plassart 34, 52 /Daniel Czap 53 /Jean-Charles Gesquière 55 /Noël Hautemanière 60, 76–7 top /Matthews 72 /Roland Huitel 92–3 /Root Stock/Hendrick Holler 106; J.-D. Sudres 110; ROUEN, musée des Beaux-Arts 113; VANVES, Explorer/F. Jalain 80–1.

Translated and adapted from the French by David Radzinowicz Howell
Copy-editing: Gillian Delaforce
Typesetting: Claude-Olivier Four
Color separation: Pollina S.A., France

Originally published as *L'ABCdaire du Vin* © 1999 Flammarion
English-language edition © 2001 Flammarion

ISBN: 2-0801-0541-8
N° d'édition: FA0541-01-V
Dépôt légal: 05/2001
Printed and bound by Pollina S.A., France - n° L83257

Pages 4–5: Pierre Victor Olagnon, *Vineyard owner visiting his winery* (detail), 1829. Beaune, musée du Vin de Bourgogne.